Bernardus de cura rei famuliaris
with some
Early Scottish Prophecies, &c.

EDITED BY

J. RAWSON LUMBY

Published for
THE EARLY ENGLISH TEXT SOCIETY
by the
OXFORD UNIVERSITY PRESS
LONDON   NEW YORK   TORONTO

FIRST PUBLISHED 1870
REPRINTED 1965

Original Series, No. 42

ORIGINALLY PRINTED BY STEPHEN AUSTIN, HERTFORD
AND NOW REPRINTED LITHOGRAPHICALLY IN GREAT BRITAIN
AT THE UNIVERSITY PRESS, OXFORD
BY VIVIAN RIDLER, PRINTER TO THE UNIVERSITY

Bernardus de cura rei famuliaris

EARLY ENGLISH TEXT SOCIETY
Original Series, No. 42
1870 (reprinted 1965)
PRICE 12s. 6d.

OXFORD
UNIVERSITY PRESS

Great Clarendon Street, Oxford OX2 6DP
United Kingdom

Oxford University Press is a department of the University of Oxford.
It furthers the University's objective of excellence in research, scholarship,
and education by publishing worldwide. Oxford is a registered trade mark of
Oxford University Press in the UK and in certain other countries

© The Early English Text Society 1870

The moral rights of the authors have been asserted

Database right Oxford University Press (maker)

First Edition published in 1870
Reprinted 1965

All rights reserved. No part of this publication may be reproduced,
stored in a retrieval system, or transmitted, in any form or by any means,
without the prior permission in writing of Oxford University Press,
or as expressly permitted by law, or under terms agreed with the appropriate
reprographics rights organization. Enquiries concerning reproduction
outside the scope of the above should be sent to the Rights Department,
Oxford University Press, at the address above

You must not circulate this book in any other form
and you must impose this same condition on any acquirer

Published in the United States of America by Oxford University Press
198 Madison Avenue, New York, NY 10016, United States of America

British Library Cataloguing in Publication Data
Data available

Library of Congress Cataloging in Publication Data
Data available

Original Series, 42

ISBN 978-0-19-722042-9

PREFACE.

THE five short pieces here printed are from a MS. marked KK. I. 5 in the Cambridge University Library. This MS., which is now broken up into several portions, is fully described in the Preface to "Ratis Raving," and it is only necessary to mention here, that the first of the following pieces is from the part of the MS. which is numbered 5, and the rest from that numbered 4.

The peculiarity of the contents, and, in the case of the paraphrase of St. Bernard and the prophecy of Beket, the uniqueness of the poems, is rather the reason for their publication than any value which attaches to the language. The poems are in the Scottish dialect, but the MS. is in a late fifteenth century hand, and the forms vary so much, either from the carelessness of the scribe, or in the case of the prophecies from the general uncertainty of the sense, that the editor deems it lost labour to enter upon a discussion of variations, for which no rule can be assigned.

In the few Notes which are appended, and in the Glossary, the pieces are distinguished by the letters A. B. C. D. E.

A. This is a paraphrase in Scottish verse of a Latin letter written by Bernard, the first abbot of Clairvaux (b. 1091—

d. 1153) to a knight named Raymund, who in the Latin is called *Castri Sancti Angeli Dominus*, but of whom I have been unable to learn anything more.

It is a compendious treatise on domestic economy, and contains advice of how to manage servants, wives, and children, as well as directions on when to spend, and when to spare.

As the Latin text, which is paraphrased, is not given completely in many cases, a reprint of the entire letter is subjoined, with various readings, enclosed in brackets, from Migne's "Bibliotheca Patrum," where the sense does not seem very clear.

Opera Sancti Bernardi Claraevallensis (Paris, 1640), column 1926.

Epistola Bernardi Sylvestris, viri quidem eruditissimi de Cura regimine rei familiaris ideo in hoc apposita volumine quod nonnulli eam a sancto Bernardo putant esse Compositam.

Gratioso et felici militi H. Raymundo castri Ambrosii, Bernardus in senium deductus salutem. Doceri petis a nobis de curâ et modo rei familiaris utilius gubernandæ, et qualiter patresfamilias debeant se habere. Ad quod tibi sic respondemus, quod licet omnium rerum mundanarum status et exitus negociorum sub fortunâ laborent non tamen sub hoc timore vivendi est regula omittenda. Audi ergo et attende quod si in domo tuâ sumptus et redditus sunt æquales, casus inopinatus poterit destruere statum ejus. Status hominis negligentis, domus est ruinosa. Quid est negligentia gubernantis domum? Ignis validus in domo accensus. Discute diligenter eorum diligentiam et propositum, qui tua administrant. Labenti enim nondum lapso facultatibus minus verecundiæ est abstinere quam cadere. Sæpius revidere quæ tua sunt, et quomodo sint, magna providentia est. Cogita de cibo et potu animalium tuorum, nam esuriunt et non petunt. Nuptiæ sumptuosæ, damnum sine honore conferunt. Sumptus pro militiâ honorabilis est. Sumptus pro juvando prodigo, perditus est. Sumptus pro juvando amicos rationabilis est. Familiam grosso cibo non delicato nutrias. Qui gulosus effectus est, vix aliter quam morte mores mutabit. Gulositas, vilis et negligentis hominis putredo est. Frugalitas, soliciti et diligentis hominis solatium est. Diebus paschalibus abundanter, non tamen delicate pasce familiam. Fac gulam litigare cum bursa, et cave cujus advocatus existas. Si autem inter gulam et bursam judex existas, sæpius sed non semper, pro bursa sententiam feras. Nam gula affectionibus probat, et sic testibus non juratis. Bursa evidenter probat, jam arcâ et cellario evacuatis, vel brevi tempore vacuandis. Tunc male judicas contra gulam quando avaritia ligat bursam. Nunquam recte inter gulam et bursam avaritia judicabit. Quid est avarus? Homicida. Quid est avaritia? Paupertatis timor, semper in paupertate vivens. Recte vivit avarus in se non perdens divitias, sed aliis reservando. Melius est enim aliis reservare quam in se perdere. Si blado abundas, non diligas caristiam : quia diligens caristiam cupit esse pauperum homicida. Vende bladum cum satis valet non quando per pauperem emi non potest. Vicinis minori pretio vende, etiam inimicis. Non semper gladio sed sæpe servitio vincitur inimicus. Superbia contra vitium, balneum [*vicinum balenum*] est expectans tonitru cum sagittâ. Habes inimicum? quæras tuum oculum pro tui custodiâ. Si habes inimicum, conversationem non habeas cum ignotis. Semper cogita quod inimicus sagax cogitat inimici vias. Debilitas inimici non est loco pacis, sed treuga ad tempus. Si te securas [*Si non es securus*] non cogitare inimicum tuum, quæ tu cogitas, periculo te exponis. De fœminis tibi suspectis quid agant, ignorantiam non sententiam quæras. Postquam sciveris crimen uxoris tuæ a nullo medico curaberis. Dolorem de malâ uxore tunc mitigabis, quando audies de uxoribus alienis. Cor nobile et altum non inquirit de operibus mulierum. Malam uxorem potius risu quam baculo castigabis. Fœmina senex et meretrix omnes divitias adnullabit. Fœmina senex et meretrix, si lex permitteret viva sepelienda esset. De vestibus. Nota quod vestis sumptuosa, probatio est pauci sensus. Vestis nimis apparens cito vicinis tædium parit. Stude bonitate placere non veste. Mulieris petitio habentis vestes et vestes quærentis, non indicat firmitatem. De amicis. Tene quod major est amicus qui sua tribuit, quam qui seipsum offert. De verbis est magna copia amicorum. Amicum non reputes qui te præsentem laudat. Si consulis amico non quæras placere ei, [*sibi*] sed rationi. Dicas in consulendo, sic mihi videtur, non præcisè, sic agendum est; quoniam facilius de malo exitu consilii redargutio sequitur, quam de bono laus. Audivi quod joculatores te visitant. Attende quæ sequuntur, Homo impendens joculatori, cito uxorem habebit, cujus nomen erit paupertas. Sed quis erit hujus uxoris filius? Derisio. Placet tibi verbum joculatoris? finge te non audire sed aliud cogitare. Ridens et gaudens de verbis joculatoris, jam pignus sibi dedit. Joculatores improperantes digni sunt suspendio. Quid est joculator mala improperans? Animal homicidium secum portans.

PREFACE.

Joculatoris instrumenta Deo non placent. Audi de famulis. Famulum alti et elati cordis repelle ut futurum inimicum. Famulum tuis moribus blandientem repelle. Famulo et vicino te præsentem laudantibus resistas aliter cogita te esse deceptum. Famulum se de facili verecundantem dilige ut filium. Si vis ædificare domum judicat [*inducat*] te necessitas, non voluntas. Cupiditas ædificandi ædificando non tollitur. Nimia et inordinata ædificandi cupiditas parit cito et expectat ædificiorum venundationem. Turris completa, et arca vacuata facuint valdè sed tardè hominem prudentem. Vis aliquando vendere : Cave cum vendere volueris, ne partem hæreditatis vendas. Non vendas potentiori sed potius minori pretio des minori : totum autem vende plus offerenti. Melius est gravem pati famem quam patrimonii venditionem. Sed melius est partem vendere, quam se usuris subjicere. Quid est usura? Venenum patrimonii. Quid est usura legis? Latro præcedens [*Legalis latro prædicens*] quod intendit. Nihil emas in consortio potentioris. Parvum consortem patienter sustineas, ne tibi fortiorem socia. Quæsivisti de usu vini. Qui in diversitate et abundantia vini sobrius est, ille est terrenus Deus. Ebrius nihil recte facit, nisi cum in lutum cadit. Sentis vinum? Fuge consortium. Sentis vinum? Quære somnum antequam colloquium. Qui se ebrium verbis excusat, ebrietatem suam aperte accusat. Male sedet in juvene vina cognoscere. Fuge medicum scientiâ plenum et exercitio non probatum. Fuge medicum ebrium. Cave tibi a medico volente in te experiri qualiter alios de simili morbo curabit. Catulos valde parvos dimitte clericis et reginis. Canes custodes utiles sunt. Canes ad venandum plus constant quam conferunt. Habes filios? Dispensatores tuorum bonorum non instituas, sed dices : Si adversetur fortuna, quid prodest vivendi doctrina? Audi quid de hoc viderim, stultorum [*stultos*] omittentes contingentia [*continentiam*], et tandem se excusantes sub fortunâ. Evenit aliquando fortuna. Sed servans doctrinam raro accusabit fortunam. Raro enim diligentiam cum infortunio sociabis sed rarius a pigritiâ infortunium separabis. Expectat piger sibi subveniri a Deo, qui in mundo isto vigilare præcepit. Tu ergo vigila, et levitatem expendendi cum gravitate lucrandi compensa. Appropinquat senectus ? Consulo quod Deo potius quàm filio tuo te committas. Disponis legata ? Consulo quod primo [*prius*] servitoribus quam sacerdotibus solvi mandes. Diligentibus personam tuam, non committas animam tuam. Committe animam tuam diligentibus suam. Dispone de rebus ante morbum. Sæpe quis efficitur infirmitatis servus et servus testari non potest : liber ergo testeris, antequam servus efficiaris. Sufficiat tibi quod de te [*testamentis*] dictum est. De filiis

PREFACE. ix

audi. Mortuo patre filii quærunt divisionem. Si nobiles sunt, melior est sæpe eorum per mundum dispersio, quam hæreditatis divisio. Nam sæpe est gravis eorum dissolutio, hujusmodi hæreditatis divisio. Si laboratores sunt, faciant quod volunt. Si mercatores sunt, tutior est eorum divisio quam communio, ne unius infortunium aliis imputetur. Mater vero, forte remaritari quærit? Stulte agit: sed ut sua peccata deploret, utinam ipsa senex accipiat juvenem. Nam non ipsam sed sua quæsivit: quibus habitis bibet cum eo doloris calicem quem optavit, ad quem perducant merita sua damnabilis senectutis.

It will be seen from the title of the above epistle that there is a doubt thrown upon its being a genuine work of St. Bernard of Clairvaux, and also that Raymund is there styled *castri Ambrosii*, which adds to the difficulty of identifying the person to whom it was sent.

B. This is a Scottish prophecy, or rather, medley of prophecies, which has been printed, though in a different order, and with many variations, in a volume published for the Bannatyne Club in 1833. The editor of that volume asserts that there can be no doubt that these "obscure and almost unintelligible rhymes must have been fabricated at a period comparatively recent."

Comparing the prophecy as here printed with the copy in the Bannatyne Club volume, we find lines 1–70 are given on pages 6, 7, and 8 with considerable variation. Lines 71, 72, are peculiar to our copy; lines 73 to 126 occur on pages 4, 5, and 6; and part of them again later on in "The Prophecie of Bertlington," pp. 14-17. Lines 127–133 are not represented in the Bannatyne copy, but 134 to the end are found on page 6. The Bannatyne reprint commences with lines which ascribe the prophecy to Merlin. With regard to the interpretation of this and the other prophecies, the editor is compelled to say "Davus sum non Œdipus." The curious in such matters are referred to a work by Alanus de Insulis (ob. 1181), entitled "Explanationes in Prophetias Merlini Angli;" and for the later allusions, to a pamphlet published

B

in 1651 by William Lilly, Student in Astrology. The title is, "Monarchy or No Monarchy in England," and the author applies passages of these prophecies to the events which had just extinguished monarchy in this country by the execution of Charles I.

C. The fragment of Beket's prophecy seems to bear upon the events of the reign of Henry V.

I have to thank Canon Robertson for the following references to passages, where it is shown that the House of Lancaster made great use of the name of St. Thomas of Canterbury in the prophecies which were circulated in the interest of their succession: Eulogium Historiarum, vol. i. pp. 406-7. Milman, Latin Christianity (ed. I.), vol. vi. pp. 96, 97. Walsingham, vol. i. p. 378; vol. ii. pp. 239, 240. Buchon, Note on Froissart, vol. xiv. p. 229.

D. The second Scottish prophecy commences with four lines similar to the initial lines of a prophecy which is printed at page 249 of vol. ii. of "Political Poems and Songs," edited by T. Wright, Esq., among the volumes published under the direction of the Master of the Rolls; the remaining ten lines of that poem are different from those which follow in our text. But it is worth while to notice that that poem consists of fourteen lines, and that in our text the fifteenth line is the commencement of a poem which has been published in the Bannatyne Club volume (p. 9), already alluded to, as a separate work, under the title of "The Prophecie of Beid." Our text corresponds in the main with that "Prophecie," down to the end of line 54, when they part company for eleven lines, which are represented by thirteen lines of the "Prophecie." The last six lines of our text are then brought in with a good deal of variation, and followed by twenty-six lines of which we have no trace.

E. This is a Scottish version of a piece printed by Caxton

as a sort of introduction to "Þe XII prouffittes or auauntages of tribulaciouns." It is printed by him with a title intimating that it is the utterances of VII wise masters; but after the title he only gives the same six opinions as are in our text.

Early Scottish Verse.

I.

[Fol. 2a.] **BERNARDUS DE CURA REI FAMULIARIS.**

  A Wtenyk bukys and ſtoris alde and new
   Be wyſz poetys ar tretit, þe quhilk trew,
  Sum maide for law of god in document,
4 And oþir ſum for varldly regiment,
  Experyence throw þam þat men may haffe
  Off ſapience, and ſa, amange þe laiffe,
  A lytil epiſtile I fande for to comende,
8 Be þe doctor bernarde, and ſende
  To raymwnde knycht of chewalry þe roſz : [1]
  Þe forme as he his howſalde ſulde contene,
  And his famele miſerabilly ſuſtene,
12 Wyt mony oþir *vir*teus eligant,
  Rycht neceſſar to vaike and ignorant.
  And quhar I ſay to lang or ȝit to ſchort,
  To pacience mekly I me report;
16 And i*n* þe nam of mary and Iheſus,
  I wyl begyne his text fyrſt ſayande þus.

Gracioso et felici militi raymundo domino castri sancti angeli Bernardus in senium deductus Salutem.

  Ande of his text fyrſt in begynynge
  To raymonde knycht he ſendys ſaluſyng.

---

[1] The line that should rhyme with this is omitted in the MS.

*Salutem et sincerem in domino caritatem. doceri petis a nobis de modo
& cura rei famuliaris gubernande, qualiter patres familias debeant se
habere: ad quod tibi respondemus, quod licet omnium rerum mundanarum status et exitus negociorum sub fortuna liborent, non tum hec
timore est viuendi regula omittenda.*

  20 Þoch alkyne ftat of varldly regiment
    Be dame fortowne, cruele and dement
    And variance, ar febyle as þe wynde,
    Ȝit rewle of lyffe is nocht to leff behynde.

Audi ergo et attende, quod si in domo tua sumptus et redditus sint equales.

  24 And fyrst prouide with werteu þat þi rent

[Fol. 2b.]   To þi expenfis be equiuolente

*Quia casus inopinatus poterit destruere statum tuum. Status hominis
negligentis est domus ruinosa.*

    For foly expenſs but temporance is noy
    And of his houſs þe ftat it may deftroy.

*Quid est negligencia gubernantis domum? ignis in domo validus et
accensus.*

  28 Qwhat is he speris þe foly negligens
    Of hym þat fulde his howfald and expenſs
    Gowerne with grace: he fayis þe man þat fpendis
    Vnfparandly mar þan his rent extendis.
  32 For as þe fyr throw brandis red ande hate
    Vaftis þe[1] felffe fa‘is he defolate.

*Discute diligenter eorum diligenciam negligenciam et propositum qui tua
administrant.*

    He fays al tyme fe thou with diligence
    Off þi feruandys haff gud experience,
  36 And þar purpoſs perfew for tyl haf plane,
    So thow confaffe gef þa be the agane
    Quhilk in þar handis haſs gouernans[2]
    Off þi gud in tyme but harme
  40 Þat þow may þam exclude.

[1] [It.]
[2] Here the rhymes are imperfect, and a line appears to be wanting, though the sense is kept up.

Labenti & nondum lapso vtile est abstinere antequam cadat, &c. Sepius reuidere que tua sunt, quom sint, maxima prouidencia est.
>This famus doctor fays it is gret prudence,
>Souerene verteu and rycht he fapience,
>Oft tyl ourefe þi gud and gouernance,
>44 Þat þow may hafe in freche remembrance
>Gef þar be ocht in perel for to fpyle :
>Of[1] ourfeynge may mende it at þi vyle
>For it is fene and faide in fampylle batht
>48 Slewthe and delay oft caufis mekyl fkatht.

Nupcie sumptuose dampnum sine honore conferunt.
>For to mak feft he fayis and hee coftage
>And fumpteuß fpenß is foly and barnage :
>[Fol. 3a.] For gef ane loffys, ane oþir difcomendys ;
>52 And tyl honowris throw feftyn few afcendis.

Sumptus pro milicia honorabilis est.
>Bot for to fpend wyt. fpenfys mefurabyle,
>For worchip is and profet honorabyl.

Sumptus pro adiuuando amicos racionabilis est.
>And for þi tendyr frende for tyl exfpende
>56 þi gudis for gud of hym is to comende.

Sumptus pro adiuuando prodigos perditus est.
>Bot for to fpende þi gude and þi fubftance
>On foly men, þat lefys by temporance,
>Proponande þat þi gud and þi vertew
>60 Sic fulechte men with worchipe fuld renew,
>Or ȝit maik rychce, lat be : for in fertane
>Owt of þe flefche wyl nocht brede in þe bane.

Considera itaque de cibo et de potu animalium tuorum nam esuriunt et non petunt.

>Se thou confyder with al þi befy cur
>64 þi beftis fude and plefe þam with pafture
>For þocht þa hunger and thryft for falt of drynk
>þa cane nocht afk, on þam þar-for thow think.

[1] [For.]

Familiam de grosso cibo & non delicato enutries.

   þi famel fede and thus fal be þar fude,
  68 Nocht delicate, fmale drynk and metis rude.
Qui gulosus effectus est vix aliter quam morte mores mutabit, &c.

   This famus clerk þus in his buk fayis he :
   Qwha is infekyt with gulofite,
   Or ȝit dedit wy$^{t.}$ wyce of drunkynneß,
  72 It leffys þam nocht quhile dede þam part dowtleß.
Gulositas vilis & negligentis hominis putredo est.

   This vofule wyce of drunkynneß þe name
   In til a man þat has na drede of fchame
   May be reput of forow and of fyne
  76 A fary fmyt tyle hyme þat leffys þar in.
Sobrietas soliciti hominis & diligentis solacium est.

[Fol. 3b.] Qwhat man delitis and haffys diligence
   On glutony to wafte and mak expence
   And haile his Joy ande folace is þar In
  80 Ande reputis fport þat wyff men reputis fyne.
Diebus paschalibus habundanter et non delicate pasce familiam tuam, &c.

   In ioyfule dayis and haly tyme pafchale
   Fede nocht þi famel with coftly victuale
   Geffe þame enwcht of drynk and metis rude
  84 Quhilk may fuffice to feruandis and þer fude
Fac gulam litigare cum bursa & caue cuius aduocatus existas, aut inter gulam et bursam qualem sentenciam feras.

   Alß he comawndis betwenß glutony
   And þi purß be ftriffe for þe maftry,
   And be fa wer al tym in thyne expenß
  88 Betwene þame twa þat thow gef rycht fentence.
   For glutony prouokys þe tyl expende
   And vaft þi gudis ; quhilk to difcomende
   þi purs þe prayis to fpende as thow may wyne
  92 Or ellis þin arthe fal be oft bare wythin.
Si autem inter gulam & bursam iudex existas, sepius, sed non semper, pro

bursa sentenciam feras. Tunc male iudicas contra gulam quom auaricia ligat bursam.

   Bot wrang iugment thow geffys and fentence blynde
    Geff auarice þi purſʒ fal lowſʒ and bynde
Nam gula affectionibus probat contra bursam, & sic testibus non iuratis : bursa euidenter probat archa & cellario vacuatis vel brevi tempore vacuandis. Nunquam inter gulam & bursam auaricia recte iudicabit.

   For glutony walde waſt þat elderys wane,
 96 And auarice walde gef noþer god na mane :
   Thare-for largeneſʒ thow tak and lef þam batht
   For he cane ſpende in tym and do na ſkatht.

Quid est auarus ? sui homicida. Quid est auaricia ? paupertatis timor : semper in paupertate viuere.

   Qwhat is, he ſperis, auarice þe fyne ?
 100 To dred purete and euer to leffe þar in.

[Fol. 4a.] *Recte viuit auarus in se non perdens diuicias, sed aliis reseruando.*

   Thar-for a wreche he leffys rycht wyſly
   In til hym felffe, and I fal tel þe quhy.
   It is aganys þe wrechiſʒ properte
 104 To ſpende, þar-for he leffys in pauperte
   And oþir men oft ſpendys þat he may wyne ;
   Þar for he leffys in forow and deis in fyne.

Melius est enim aliis reseruare quam in se perdere.

   Bot better is to oþir kepe þi pelffe
 108 Þan to forſwme and waſt away þi felffe.

Si habundas blado non diligas caristiam : diligens caristiam cupit esse pauperum homicida.

   Geff thow be rycht man of gouernance,
   And hafe to fel wetale in gret fubſtance,
   Se be na way na derth þat thou defyre
 112 For þi wynnyng for dred of goddis Ire :
   Thow cowattyſʒ þane, planly I þe aſſur,
   To be oppreſſer and ſlaar of þe pur.

Vende bladum tuum dum satis valet non quando per pauperem emi non potest.

Mane, fel þi corne and alſȝ þi victuale
116 For mefurabyl vynnynge profet and awale,
And in þat tym defyr for to fel nocht,
Qwhen be þe pur na way it may be bocht.

Vicinis minore precio vende etiam inimicis. Non gladio sed sepe seruicio vincitur inimicus.

And to þi nychtbowr, as refone is and ſkyle,
120 Sel better chepe na thow oþir tyle:
And to þi fayis gud chepe, prente þis worde,
For he is nocht ay wencufte with þe fworde
But oft throw lufe and dedys of cheryte.
[Fol. 4b.] 124 Ande lawlyneſȝ ourcummyne oft his he.

Superbia contra vicinum habere balteum est expectens tonitruum cum sagitta.

Se thow be fobyr ande ber þe, man, ewynli
To þi nychbowr þat dwellis þe ner by.
And in þi harte inwy þam nocht throw pryde;
128 For and thow do dowtleſȝ, mane, confyde,
It is þe fendys prouocacione
Takyne of noy ande tribulacione.

Habens inimicum conuersacionem non habeas cum ignotis sed cogita inimici tui vias.

Geff þat it happynnis throw rancor or Inwy
132 The for to haf a dedly inimy,
It is na wyt, na wertu fekyrli,
For to conwerſȝ wyth ftrangeris inwartly.
To þe of cafe, for it may happyn fa,
136 Sum mane is frende til hyme þat is þi fa

Debilitas in inimici non est loco pacis sed treuga ad tempus.

On þe gef þat þi mortale inimy
For cauſȝ may nocht fchaw furtht his felony
He bydis his howre þat he may be þi bane
140 Ande quhile his tym hys trewis þai ar bot tane.

De feminis tuis suspectis quid agant ignoranciam queras. Postquam sciueris crimen male uxoris a nullo medico curaberis.

This doctor fayis off wyfdome in his faw,
Quhat fum euer mane happynnis for to knaw
þe wykytneſſ and forow of a wyfe,
144 Na medicine may mende hyme in his lyffe,
Na þe dolowr of hyr þat is his make
[Fol. 5a.] Be na fcience þar is na leche can flake.

Dolorem de mala muliere tunc mitigabis quando audies facta de vxoribus alienis.

Bot it wyl flak fum part of fꝏrowis fer
148 Of oþir wyffys þe forow for to her,
And mare fobyr to thole fic vikytneſſ,
Mane, to confaife þat þow art nocht makleſſ.

Cor altum et nobile non inquirit de operibus mulierum.

Bot nobyl hartis ande gentyl fettys nocht by
152 Off wice and verkys quhilk ar wnwomanly.
For þa confaue þat womannys wyttis ar thyne
And noch[t] fa abyl to werteu as to fyne:
Quhilk cummys þam of kynde and of nature
156 Of þar formodyr eua þat þam bure.

Malam uxorem pocius risu quam baculo castigabis.

This nobyl clerk fays thow fal foner fefe
Of ewyl women þe forow þan be pefe
Quhen þat þai chide and chauner for to lacht
160 Na bet with ftaffeis quhile þa ly by þe wacht.

Femina meretrix & senex si lex permitteret sepelienda esset viua, &c.

This doctor fays, ane aulde woman þat is
Licherus and wyl not lef hir myſſ,
And law wald thole hir for to perfewere
164 Nan oþir hewyne fcho walde neuer eftyr fper,
Thocht elde be cummyne ande paffit al hir flowris
Ʒit walde fcho luffe and be luffyt paramowris.

Si securum putas inimicum vt supra.

Man, of þi fa gef thow hafe ony dowte,
168 Be wakyr al tyme and war þe abowte,

BERNARDUS DE CURA

    þe to conferffe with vertu fra his ile
[Fol. 5b.] Wycht fobyrneſs ſtedfasſtly and ſtyle.

De vestibus vero teneas. Vestis sumptuosa est probacio pauci sensus, &c.

    Off clethyng now þis clerk wyl fpek a fpase.
172 Coſtly clething fe[1] fais is wantonafe,
    Off lityle wyt to men of fympil ſtate,
    Off mefwre ay he byddis the halde þe gate

Vestis nimis apparens vicinis tedium parat.

    For ryche aray and freche apparalyne
176 Dois oft tymis ſkath, & principaly in þis thing :
    Nychbouris abowt wyl fay in þar entent,
    Loo fe fo gay ȝon man is of his rent !
    And þe in hart þar-for þa hewy ber.
180 Eftyr þi wyne with worfchipe clethyng wer.

Stude ergo bonitate non veste placere.

    Bot erare sone þe forſs at al þe power
    To pleſs gudneſs and gud be callit her.
    That men may say, ȝon man is of renowne,
184 þat is bettyr na for to ruſs þi gowne.

Mulieris peticio habentis vestes & vestes quærentis non indicat firmitatem.
De amicis tene quod maior est amicus qui sua tribuit quam qui seipsum offert, &c.

    Off frendys þus þis doctor cane decide ;
    In to þat frende erar thow confyde
    Quhilk the fupportis in þi neceffite,
188 Na in hym fays, al myn frend fal be
    Chargis me at al ȝour owne I am fekyr.
    þar is nocht ellis bot ioly wordis as þir.

Nam de verbis magna est copia amicorum.

    Bot mony frendis to nowmer ar be tale,
192 In to þir wordis bot few in fpeciale.
[Fol. 6a.] *Amicum non reputes qui te presentem laudat.*
    Man, reput nocht hym frende quhilk in þi face
    Gyffis grei lowynge and fais þow art makleſs.

            [1] [he].

Confaffe fic glofs and al fic fenȝit fere
196 In to þi hart and in þi breft thow bere,
And traft hyra nocht, fuppofs he were þi brudyr,
Bot gef a ioly worde ay for ane vdyr.

Si consolis amico non queras placere ei sed rationi.

Sone to þi frend gef thow fal gef confele,
200 For his profet honowr ande awale,
As refone afkys þi confel gef hym tyl,
And folow nocht his plefance na his vyle.

Dicas in consulendo amico, sic mihi videtur, non precise, sic agendum est, &c.

Alfs be þi frend in way of confellyng
204 Geffe thow be chargit gef it but fenȝeing
How he fal doo but dowt determinatly,
And difcufs nocht his mater miftely.

Facilius enim de malo exitu consilii sequitur redargucio quam de bono laus, &c.

For ofterfyfs reprwfe and welany
208 And ewyle confele folowis mare fodanly
Þan doys loffyng or comendacione
Of trew confel or gud prouifione.

Audiui quod visitant te ioculatores; audi que sequuntur, &c.

Man or childe haffande a gret delyte
212 For to wefy with diligence perfit
Ioculatouris or trumpouris, fone, attende
Quhat falowis eftyr or quhat fal be þe ende.

Homo ioculatoribus intendens & impendens cito habebit uxorem cuius nomen erit paupertas, & erit huius uxoris filius derisio.

[Fol. 6b.]   A mane, he fays, quhik al his fantafy
216 Has geffyne to vice and vefy ioculary,
A wyfe he fal hafe, purte til hir name,
And a fone alfs callit fcorne and fchame.

Placent tibi verba ioculatoris finge te audire et aliud cogitare, &c.

Gef quhillumys plefeis ioculatoris, my dere,
220 Fenȝe þe þar fantafy to here

Bot lat þi mynde and þine inwart entent
On odyr materſ be ſade and diligent.

Ridens & gaudens de verbis ioculatoris Jam pignus sibi dedit.   Ioculatores improperantes digni sunt suspendio, &c.

A mane to lach at ioculatouris fantaſy,
224 It is rewarde to þam, ſone, ſekyrli,
And pryſeis þat a gyft of gudly price
For it foſteris and rutis þam in þar vice.

Quid est ioculator mala improperans ? anime homicidium secum portans, &c.

Quhat is, he ſays, a ioculatour, late ſee,
228 A mane inclinande to iniquite,
Ande of his ſaule a ſlaar ſekyrli
Ande mony oþiris throw his falſ fantaſy.

Ioculatores instrumenta nunquam deo placuerunt.

The inſtrumentis pertenande ioculary
232 War neuer pleſande to god ȝeit ſekyrly.

Audi de famulis: famulum alti cordis repelle ut futurum inimicum.

This nobyle doctor to þe he wyl declare,
Qwhat kynde of ſeruande is familier,
That ſeruande, ſone, quhilk has a hart of pryde
236 In þi ſeruice thou thole hym nocht to byde,
Bot fra þe ſone þat ſeruande thou exclude
[Fol. 7a.]   As inimys þe quhilk walde the na gud.

Famulum tuis moribus blandientem repelle.

Þa ſeruandys, ſone, þe quhilk ar in þar langagis
240 Thow felis flech ſchawand a far viſagis,
In tym be wer, ſone, for þar ſutelte
For ſeruandis þa ar batht falſ and ſle.

Famulo et vicino te laudantibus resiste, aliter cogita te esse deceptum.

That ſeruande ſone I rede thow cheſ nocht alſ
244 Þat loffys þe in þi face, he is falſ,
For wyrk thow oder wnwerteuſly or vele
All is done weile þat ſchrew ſweris be his ſele.

Famulum de facili verecundantem dilige ut filium.

Bot þat ſeruande, my ſwet ſone, thow cheſ
248 Þe quhilk ſchamys with his myſdeide þou ſeis,

And argewis no*ch*t agane pre*f*umptuu*f*ly,
No in þi charg*is* *f*chawis na p*r*ophe*f*y,
As gef thow *f*ayis, o *f*eruande, feche me þis,
252 He *f*ayis, *f*on, al redy *f*chir I wyſs,
Bot he þat pa*ff*is with murm*ur* and a *f*ang
And wyl no*ch*t get it he wat weil or he gang,
Serve nequ*am* þat childe to nam has tane,
256 Now in þis varlde of *f*ic is mony ane.

Vis edificare: ad edificandum inducat te necessitas et non voluntas.

How *f*al thow byg ca*f*tel towne or toure
This clerk he ke*n*nys, or lytil hal or bowr*e*,
Thow prent i*n* hart fyr*f*t þi nece*ff*iite
260 And of how*f*eis quhat may *f*uffice the
And lat thou no*ch*t þi wyl and wantona*f*ſ
Con*f*um þar-one þi *f*ub*f*tance and rycha*f*ſ.

Cupiditas edificandi edificando non tollitur, &c., &c.

[Fol. 7b.] Gef thow cowat*is* to byg with gret de*f*yr,
264 Ʒeit biggyne haue no*ch*t þi cowatynge ex*f*pire,
þe mar þow art applyit to poli*f*y
The mare encre*f*eis þi mynde i*n* fanta*f*y.

Nimia & inordinata edificandi cupiditas expectat edificiorum vendicionem.

Sumpteu*f*ſ biggyne inordinat and hee
268 It is bot bydyne of *f*ellyn thow may *f*e
Off tenement*is* and biggynis ryche agane :
For halffe þe golde to geff þam men ar fane.

Turris edificata & completa & archa vacuata vel brevi tempore vacuanda-
faciunt valde sed tarde hominem sapientem.

Thi tenement complet and con*f*u*m*mat,
272 Thyne *f*ilu*er* and þ*i*ne arch euacuate,
It makys quhill trew towris he of price
þar-for thow byg na mar na wyl *f*uffice.

Vis aliquid vendere caue ne vendas partem hereditatis tue potenciori
te sed pocius minori precio des minori.

For mi*f*tyr ge*f*e it happy*i*nis þe to *f*el
276 Thyne heritage to quham *f*one, I *f*al tel.

Wyth mychti men fe þat thow haf na dale
þoth þai promyt þe twif for it þe wale.
In myftir quhen þe nedis for to hafe
280 þa wil difplefȝ þam at þe and thou crafe.
To gudly men thow fel þi land and gud
þan nedis thow nocht to rewerfȝ hate na hude,
To crafe þine awne bot haf it at þi wyl.
284 Sone, for lefȝ price þi thing fel fic men tyl.

Totum autem vendas plus offerenti.

And louandly wyth verteu fel þi lande
Til hym geffis mafte and tak it in þi hande.

Melius est grauem pati famem quam patrimonium vendicionem.

[Fol. 8a.]   Sone, bettyr is to fuftene hungir gret
288 And greft fkantnefȝ, fone, batht of drink & met
Na for to fel þine herytagis and lande
þe quhilk þi fadyr fefeit in þi hand.

*Sed melius est partem vendere quam vsuris subicere. Quid est vsura?
venenum patrimonii. Quid est vsurarius? legalis latro predicens quod
intendit. Nichil emas in consorcio potenciorum.*

Sone, drefȝ þe nocht na marchandifȝ to by
292 Of mychti men in to þe company.

Paruum consortem pacienter sustineas, ne tibi sorciat forciorem.

Gyf a fmale frend it hapynnis þe to haue,
Or a falow þou luffys our þe laffe,
Se þow fuftene and thole hym paciently,
296 Thocht he excede fum tyme rekleſly.
For fuld it happyn þe hym til exclude
Perawentour þu wal nocht get fa gude.

*Quesisti de vsu vini. qui in duersitate et habundancia vinorum est
sobrius, ille est quasi terrenus deus.*

A mane, fe[1] fays, of wyne þat has vfage
300 Ande habundance and fyne is nocht faffage
Thow mychtinefȝ and confort of þe wyne
At temporance bydis and fobyr fyne ;

[1] [he.]

It is a gyft of grace and god abufe
304 Sende fra þe hewyne in to þat man for luffe.

Ebrietas nichil recte facit nisi cum in lutum cadit.

Schir drunkyineſs þat fyre doys no thing rych[t],
Thocht falomon he be and fampſone wycht,
Ande quhilis a nape to mak mowis as a fule,
308 Bot as a fow quhen he fallis in a pule.

Sentis vinum ? fuge consorcium, quere somnium pocius quam colloquium.

[Fol. 8b.] Perfaweis þu þe lycht of wyne and blycht?
Fra company my fwet fone draw þe fwycht,
To þi chalmer to beek þi nape is beft.
312 Litil of langage be þan bot tak þe reft.

Qui se ebrium verbis excusat suam ebrietatem a parte accusat, &c.

Quhat fum euer man excufeis reklefneſs
Of worde and verk with fchyr drunkynneſs,
He accufeis hym felffe and his foly,
316 As wnwyfmane þat temperance gayis by.

Male sedet in Juuine vinum cognoscere.

It cordis il in ȝouthhede of a childe
Off tendyr age, or ȝit in madyne mylde,
Diuersiteis of wynis for to knaw,
320 And þar gudneſs, for þat wyl viceis draw.

Fuge medicum ebrium.

In to þe handys put nocht þi hape and hele,
Sone, of þat leche with drunkynneſs cane dele.

Caue tibi a medico volenti in te experiri qualiter alios de simili morbo curabit. &c.

Caniculos valde paruos dimitte clericis et reginis.

Litile doggis and meffanys with þar bellis
324 To clerkis and qweynis cordis and to non ellys.

Canes pro custodia vtiles sunt.

Bot wakyr doggis ar profitabyl to fede
To kepe þi hale one nycht gef þu has nede.

Canes ad venandum plus constant quam conferunt.

D

Bot hwndis gret to fed to hwnte on felde
328 Ar coftlyar þan þa wyl mak ganȝelde.

Habentem filios dispensatorum bonorum tuorum non instituas, &c.

Haf þow fonnis, for confel I conclude,
Thow mak þam nocht difponeris of þi gude,
[Fol. 9a.] Perauentowr throw flewcht and negligence
332 Or wanfortowne or wnganand expence
Thow waxis pur, þane fortone wil þe wyt,
And haf na dantetht of þi fone na delite,
Bot fay quhat profettis þis reid of lif to lere
336 For murmur man difpone þi gud and ger.

Sed tu dicas si aduersetur fortuna, quid prodest viuendi doctrina. Audi quid de hoc viderim. Stultos obnitentes contingenciam & se excusantes sub fortuna, eorum infortunium aliis imputantes, vidi facultatibus cito labi, &c.

Sone, foly menne quhilk ar inoportwne,
Quhen þa wax pure, throw þar flewcht wil fay fone
Quhat kynde of ftat may fortowne be agane,
340 Bot þis doctryne to kepe and þu þe pane
þi fpirit fal and befyneſ accoufe
Fortowne and þow wil nocht þi gud abwſ.

Raro enim diligenciam cum infortunio sociabis, sed rarius a pigricia infortunium sociabis.

For feldyne, fone, befy diligence
344 Folowis with wanfortonys violence :
Bot feldinar wanfourtowne þu deffewyr
Sale fra fwerneſ, quhilk de na wirk had leuer.

Expectat piger sibi subueniri a deo qui vigilare precepit in mundo, &c.

For fchyr fwerneſ to vyrke he wyl fone tyre
348 And cryis one god quhen he lyis in þe myre
Hyme for to helpe, bot helpe hyme felff no wyle
Bot quhil god cum and tak hym upe lys ftile,
Quham god of mycht bade wald and virke & leffe
352 In wytneſ of adame and of eue.

Tu ergo vigila et leuitatem expendendi cum grauitate lucrandi compensa, &c.

[Fol. 9b.] Tharfor, o mane and wrechyte creatowr
Maide in þis warlde dolowr to endour,
Be wyſƷ and were and walkyr for to wyne
356 Thi liffys fude but det and dedly ſyne,
Expendande ay þi wynnyng and rycheſƷ
Be ewyne compenſƷ to þe ſwet of þi face
And forſum nocht þi weilefar viciuſly
360 Syn wyt fortowne and thow þi ſelffe gilty.

Appropinquat senectus : consulo quod deo pocius quam tuo filio te committas, &c.

Qwhen febyle elde has tane þe throw his dat,
And þi ſpretis vax dul and blat,
Errer to god þi ſaul þi ſelff commit
364 Nay to þi ſone þow ded to do for it.

Disponis legata : consulo quod primo seruitoribus quam sacerdotibus solui mandes, &c.

Gef thow dyſponis and leffys legaſy
In fyrſt thow pay þi ſeruandis, confel I,
For haly wyrt ſayis þat ſeruandis fee
368 Wnpayit wengeance cryis to þe hewyne one hee.

Diligentibus personam tuam non committas animam tuam, &c.

Commyt þᵘ nocht þi ſawle in to þer handis
Þat luffys the to bryng it owt of bandis.

Committe animam tuam diligentibus animam suam.

Bot in þar handys þi ſawle thow ſal comende
372 Þat luffys þar ſaule, for ſic mene may it mende.

Dispone de rebus tuis ante morbum. Sepe enim quis efficitur infirmitatis seruus & seruus testari non potest. liber ergo testeris antequam seruus efficiaris.

In freche memor befor Infirmyte
Thow ſulde diſpone and lefe legaſye
For quhen ſekneſƷ abowte þi hart is plet,
376 Thy mynde þi ſawle to god þan ſulde be ſet.

[Fol. 10a.] Ande paynnys gret with ſchowrys ſcharpe amange
Cauſeis þi wyt to wauer and ga wrange.

De filiis autem audi, &c.

This nobyl clerke now wyl he ſpek a ſpace
380 Of ʒonge childyr quhilk ar left fadyrleſꝫ.
Mortuo patre querunt diuisionem filii.
And fyrſte, he faẏs, þe fadyr beande dede,
Oftſyſꝫ þe ſone flittys to fremyt ſted.
Si nobiles sunt melior est eorum per mundum dispersio quam hereditatis diuisio.
And fyne he fays gef þer progenitouris
384 War nobyl men, gentyl and of valouriſꝫ,
Haffande liflate and land in herytagis,
Better is ſtalynge of þar barnagis
In to þe warlde to gowerne be þer grace
388 Na to dewyde þar herytagis dowtlaſꝫ.
Si vero sunt laboratores faciunt quid volunt.
And gef þer faderis war feruandis or hwſbandis,
Lat þam ga feike fic laboris in þe landis,
Batht tel and faw and dyk and delff þe erde,
392 Or vfe fum craft as geffyne it to þam verde.
Si mercatores tucior est diuisio eis quam communicacio ne vnius infortunium aliis imputetur.
And gef þar·faderys be marchande men of mycht
And tile ilk barne dewydis his rycheſꝫ rycht,
Be hiis powr ilkane a porcione
396 Better is of þam diuifione
And of þar guddys batht be fe ande lande
þane may nane fic vnhap til oþeris hande.
Mater vero 'tua senex forte remaritari querit, stulte agit, sed vt peccata sua deploret,
Thar moderis þan defyris mariage
400 Quhilk is wanwyt and foly in þar age.
[Fol. 10*b*.] *Vtinam ipsa senex maritum accipiat iuniorem qui non ipsam sed que sua sunt querit quibus habitis & deuastatis bibet cum ea calicem doloris quem optauit ad quem eam perducunt merita sue dampnabilis senectus. Amen.*
But mare þar moderis in elde wyl mary þane
To fpende þar gudys bryngis hame a fwet ʒong mane,

Quhilk mary þane bot for þar gud ande ger,
404 Qwhen þat is gane, þar is bot leftande wer.
For eu*er* day þane wyl þa fecht and flyt:
Sic ful women þar wantoneß may wyt,
þat can nocht leffe in lykyne þam alane:
408 Be this vertew na fampylle may be tane.

Those who marry for money only live in strife when it is gone.

Et sic { *Explicit tractus bernardi de cura rei famuliaris, &c.* } *est finis.*

II.

ANCIENT SCOTTISH PROPHECY, No. 1.

[Fol. 25a.]
When the Cock of the North bids his birds fly,

Q When the koke in the northe halows his neft,
And bufk*is* his birdys and bunnys to flee,
Þan fhall fortune his frende þe ȝatt*is* vpcafte,
4 And Rychte fhall haue his Free entre;
Then þe mone fhall Ryfe in the northweft
IN A clowde als blak as the bill of A crawe:

the Lion shall be loose, and a Dragon shall help him.

Þen fhall the lyonne be louffe, þe baldeft & beft
8 Þat eu*er* was in brattane fen i*n* Arthuris dayes.
A dredfull dragoune fhall dreffe hime fro his den
To helpe the lyonne wyth all his myghte:
A bull and A baftarde fperys to fpend
12 Shall abyde wyghe þe bere and Rekyn his Ryght.

A Leopard shall rise in the South.

A libert engendret of a native kynde
Wyght the fterne of bedleme fall Ryfe in þe fouth;
The mole & þe marmadyne movyde in mynde,
16 Cryft þat Is our creatour has curfede be mouth:
The Egyll and þe antelope fall baldly abyde,
And Sadilles horfe, and a bore wygh bernyfe fo brycht.

At Sandyfurde shall a battle be, fulfilling Thomas's prophecy,

At Sandyfurde, for-futhe, in þe fouth fyde,
20 A pruude prunce in þe prefe lordly fall lythe,
Wycht balde bernefe in bufhment þe batell fall mete:
Þar fall profecy proffe þat thomas of tellys;
Mony A comly knyghte fall be caft und*er* fute,

and many a maiden and wife shall mourn.

24 Þat fall make maydene to wepe þat in bour duellis:
Þen fall dulefull deftany drive to þe nyghte;
Mony wyff and maydene in mornynge fall be brocht.

  Þar fall mete on morne wyghte mone lyghte;   *Betwixt Se-*
28 Be-tuix Setone and þe See forow fall be wrought.   *ton and the*
  Be þar þe lyonne fall be hurte, bot nocht perichede be,   *sea shall be the fight:* [Fol. 25b.]
  He fall brayde to þe beft þat hime þe wound wrought,   *the Lion shall be hurt, and*
  And mony fterne in þat ftoure fhall fale for þat fre,   *attack the beast that*
32 And þe proudefte in þat prefe wycht ball has it bought.   *wounded him.*
  Þe fox and þe fowmerte in alfʒ fall be tane,   *He shall judge the*
  And to þe lyonne be lede, þe law tyll abyde.   *Fox and Fulmart,*
  Bothe þe puppede and þe pye fall fuffre þe fame,   *the Puppede, Pie, and the*
36 And all þe frendis off þe fox fall fall fra þere pryde.   *friends of the Fox.*
  Then fall tro vntrew tremyll that day   *The untrue shall trem-*
  For drede of the dede man when þai her hime fpelk,   *ble;*
  And þe comoynis of kynt fall kaft hime key,
40 The bufment of brykhyll þer-wyth fall breke.
  When Wenoum and wadis ar waftyd & away lede,   *and when Venom is*
  And euerylk feede in his fefoune kyndly fett,   *banished, and right*
  And ilk Ryght has his Rewyll, and falfhede fled,   *rules, we shall have*
44 We fall haue plente of pefe when law has no lett,   *peace and plenty.*
  All grace and gudenes fall grow ws amonge,
  And euerylk freytt fall haue foyfoune be land & be See.
  The fpoufe of cryft wytht Jocounde Sange
48 Thank we gode þar-of in trinite.
  Then þe fonn & þe mone fall fhine full brycht,   *The sun and moon shall*
  Þat mony longe day full dirke has beyne,   *no longer be dark.*
  And kep þar courfe both day and nycht
52 Wyth moo myrthis þen mene may meyne.
  Þen the lyonne wytht the lyoniffes efter þat fall Reigne;   *The Lion and Lionesses*
  Þus bretlingtone bukis and banftre tellis,   *shall reign, as Bannister,*
  Merlyne and mony moo þat mene of may mene,   *Merlin, Wig-*
56 And þe expofitoris Wigythtoune & thomas wytht-all tell.   *ythtoun and Thomas say.*
  Sone at þe Saxonis fall chefʒ þame a lorde,
   And full fone bryng hyme at vnder.   *[Fol. 26a.]*
  A ded man fall make A corde
60 And þat fall be full mekyll wonder.
  He þat Is dede ande beryde in fyght,   *The dead shall rise and*
   Sall Ryfe ayane, and lyffe in lande,   *live*

to comfort a Knight	In comforte of A yhong knyght
	64 þat fortoune has fchofe to be hir hufbande.
	The whelle fall turne to hime full Ryght
whom Fortune chooses.	þat fortune has choffin to be hir fer;
He shall fight in Syria,	IN Surry he fall fhew A fyght,
	68 And in babylone bringe mony on one ber;
	Fyftyne dayis Iornay fro Ierufoleme
and win the Holy Cross.	þe haly croffe wyne fall hee:
	þe fame bore fall bere þe beme
	72 And yhit fall it fayle in the fyrft þat þe frek thinkis.
	Whenne þe kokke cane craw, kepe well his came,
The Fox and Fulmart are both false.	For þe fox and þe foulmert þai ar botht falfʒ.
	Qwhene þe Rawne and the Ruke has Rowned to geder,
	76 þen the kyng in his kytht fall acorde fame:
	þen fall þai be boulde, and bow fonefter:
The Bull shall bellow.	Then þe bull in bollingtime fall make A gret bere;
	It Is bot wynde þat he vawes, for he is bot away.
War shall rise;	80 þen fall vakne vp A were, and mekyll waa efter
	When þe bernys of þe Rawme Ruggis & Revys:
	þen þe lell men of lowthyane lepis on þar horfʒ,
the poor shall be spoiled, and the Abbeys on Tweed.	And þe pure pepill falbe fpoyled full nere.
	84 Bot the merfʒ fall murne mony day efter,
	And þe abbays trewly þat ftandis on twede.
	And all lell men fall lyff þame on þar lyffis awnter,
[Fol. 26b.]	þai fall Ruee and byrne, and mekyll Reveryfe make.
	88 þan dar no pur man fay whofe man he is,
	þan fall þat lande be lawlefʒ, for luf is þar nane;
Falsehood shall rule five years.	þan fall falffet haue fute fully V. yhere,
	And treuth trewly falbe tynt and few traft oþir,
	92 Bot for to gette of his gudes he myght thole hime gone.
A peace shall be tried, but shall not last,	þen þai fall call A counfell for pefe of þat kyth,
	To mak luf among lordis bot þat fall nocht left,
	þar falbe Baronys and bachelres þat wyll nocht obey;
	96 Rar wyll nocht kepe þar crye nor come to þar call.
and punishment shall soon come.	þen sall men be merkyt for þar myfdede,
	þat fall turne þame to teyne wyght-in fchort tume efter:

Fra xiij be paſſede and þen twiſe thre,
100 Þe tripe is þan faſtly at ane oynde :
Þe Gayt buke þat mayde þe greyfe is þen ner gone,
IN A watter he ſall abyde, and he ſall fey worth;
In his fayre foreſt ſall ane ern bygge,
104 And mony on ſall tyne þir lyff in the mene tyme :
Þai ſall founde to þe felde, and þen ferſly fyght,   *A battle shall be fought on a broad moor.*
Apone A brode mure þar ſall A batell be,
Be-ſyde a ſtob croſe of ſtane þat ſtandis on A mure :
108 It ſall be coueret wyght corſis all of a kynth,
That þe craw ſall nocht ken whar þe croſſ ſtandis.
Þe wouff ſalbe wachmane and kep mony wayis,   *The Wolf shall be true to the Lion,*
And ſall be lell to þe lyonne & loue bot hime allone.
112 Haly kyrke ſall be couerit and be beſt in þat kynth,
Wyth ledys þat lewis nocht on cryſt ; bot þat ſall nocht left.
Fra bambrwgh to þe baſſe on the brayde See,   *and from Bamborough [Fol. 27a.]*
And fra farnelande to the fyrth ſalbe a fayr ſygh
116 O barges and ballungerys, and mony brod ſayle :
And the lybberte with the flurdowlyſʒ ſall fayr þer apon.   *shall the Leopard with the Fleur-de-lys sail.*
Þar ſall A huntter in hycht come fra the Southe   *A hunter from the South shall walk over the Forth, and win a fight in Fife,*
Wyght mony Rechis on Raw Rewleyd full Ryght,
120 And he ſall fayr on his fute our the watter of forth.
Þan in fyfe he ſall fycht, and the fyld wyne ;
And the chiftanis ſall dye on þe twin halffis :
Qwhen þe man and þe mone is moſt in his mycht,
124 Þen ſall dunbertone turne vp þat is doune,
And þe mounte of Arane, bath at þat tume.
Þe lede wych lukyne haue þat lede ſall he loſʒ,
And mony on full doughty ſall dye for þat dede ;   *and many a doughty man shall die.*
128 And mony lede of þe North ſall þar lyffis loſſe,
And mony merchauntis ſall murne for A mane ache
Þat ſall turne þam to teyn wyth-in ſchort time efter ;
& þat Ilka wynttyr A ferly ſall fall,   *That winter shall many lords perish, when Tarburt crags fall into the sea.*
132 Mony of þe lordis of þat land þar lyffis ſall loſſ
For couatyſe and treſoune þat time in the lande,
Qwhen the craggis of tarbart tumleſʒ in þe Se,

E

Bede and Bannister say so. Merlin, alas, has been shut up in a Cornwall crag.

At the next Som*er* eft*er* forow for eu*er*.
136 For bed*is* buke haue I feyn, & banyfters als;
And m*er*welus merlyn*e* is waftede away
Wyght A wykede womane,—woo mycht fho bee!—
Scho has clofede him in A cragge of cornwales cofte.

III.

FRAGMENT OF AN ALLITERATIVE POEM CONTAINING THOMAS A-BEKET'S PROPHECIES.

. . . .

THomas takes the Iuell,—and Ihesus thankis,— [Fol. 27b.]
þat comyne was to hume fro his Ientyll moder.

Als bekat bad at his meffe, now has a boy ftone
4 þe brydylle of his blonke hede, agayne he bufke fhulde.
þai turnyt to Thomas, and hume þis tale taulde.
"Love barnes," quod beket, "go by me ane oþer;
For the falffede fall fayr, Safell fall fall to the erth,
8 And falbe al to-Rokked wyth Rude wederys Ruth to þe grounde;
Forthy wende we on oþir ways, and hime no more wroth;
For all þar wroke fall ende wyght þam felwne."

Thus he windes on his way, (wyffe hume our lorde!)
12 Twelff days Iurnay, as the buke tellys;
At the laft he landes in ane noþer lande, þer avyoune ftandis.
Thomas knelyde downe on his kne, and keffed the grunde,
And gat vp A glowe full of that grunde wyth glayde hartis,
16 And fayde to þerles fone of waryn, "it is worth all, and mekyll ȝelde,"
"Be my faule," he fayde, "þat war a Selly, þat ar Riall and Rewme,"
"Yis," fays thomas, els war a Selly, [. . . . . ¹]
For her Sall þe pope of Rome fett, and his See halde.

[Fol. 27b.] Beket takes his mother's jewel [? the Book of Prophecy]; and as a boy has stolen his bridle, orders another to be bought.

He journeys twelve days, lands where Avyoune is, and tells Lord Waryn's son

that the Pope of Rome shall sit there.

¹ The defective alliteration here shows that half a line is omitted.

POEM ON THOMAS A-BEKET'S PROPHECIES.

20 þis caytiwe auoyoune, þat na man now kepis,
Heder fall kyng and clerk cayr for helpe ;
And full fayne be to feche fude for þar Saulys ;

The place shall be taken for a town, and wonders shall happen.
þe vernycle of Rome fall full anerly be wyde.
24 þis fall be tane for A towne, and nocht be tentyde,
And þen fall ferlis feell fall on þe warlde.
He þat is Rewler of refone fall neuer Reke of it,
Bot lat Rewmes and Ryche lordes Rufche to geþer ;
28 All for faute of A fader fall feell folk dye."

[Fol. 28a.]
Beket goes on to Poitou, sups at a burgess's house with Waryn and Wake,
Thomas paffis furthe, ande A paffe haldis,
Tyll he come to payters throw perlyhous wais.
He bufkis tyll A burges houfe, quhar hime beft thocht,
32 And fet tyll hime tyll his Super wyth vj. lordis childer ;
He hayd no power in his purs to pay for lyk clerkis,
Bot wyth þe waryn and þe wake hamwerde he wendis ;
For þai fand hime at the courte, þai kend hime better ;
36 A porer prelet thane thomas was paffede neuer of Englonde.

and asks the burgess "who owns a work þere, set out for a tower,
Thomas afkede þe hufbande wytht full hende wordis ;
" And fer, and þi wyll war, wete wald I fayne,
Qwha is mayftr of yhon werk þat is tyll A tour merkyt ;
40 Me think it is harme, be hewine, that it no helpe has ;
For war it byggod up," quod beket, "your towne war the better,

which the town wants on the west."
For ony way that mycht happine, on yon weft halfe."

"King Charles ordered the tower, but the workmen found a letter on a stone, saying,
" Sir clerk," sayis the cleyn burges, " be cryft I fall the tell :
44 Kyng charlef our cheiffe chefyde him felwen,
He walde haue tried vp A toure, gyff ony tuyll Rafe ;
Þen was þer Suilk A Selly fewne in þe fame time,
þai fand A fayr letter on A ftone faft,
48 þat it wonderrede all the werkmen þat þe werk wroght ;
It fayd, ' mafterles men, yhe this tour make ;

'A Boar from Britain shall root up your tower and town.'
A Bayre fall come out of Berttane wytht fo brode tufkis,
He fall trauyll up yhour towre, and your towne þer efter,
52 And dycht his den in þe derreft place þat euer aucht kynge charl[es.]'

POEM ON THOMAS A-BEKET'S PROPHECIES.

This foulkes had ferly þeroffe, and the [freke]¹ fechede ;   *So they sent for the Wise Man,*
He herd it full Rathly, and Rewyde fone efter.
He keſt the ſtone in þe watter, & bad it waa worghe ;
56 And fayde, 'Maſouns, be fant mary, no mor fall yhe make.   *and he bade them stop their work.*
Bot what wy þat it wynnis, ger werk yt hime fellwyn.'
For-thy it is grathly grathede, and þe ground þus lewyde ;   *They did; and we dread the Boar."*
And we hynge in A hop, for drede of the bayre."   [Fol. 28b.]

60 And þon knelys thomas downe, & call tyll our lady ;   *Beket asks our lady whether the Boar shall come from Britain.*
"Der lady, latte me witt, (and thy wille were,)
Qwheþer of berttaine þat is braide, fall þis ber Ryfe."
The bleſſyt lady bounnede hyme to, and bleſſed hime for euer ;
64 "Beket," ſcho fayde, "be balde, þi buke it tell the beſt ;   *She says yes.*
It is the gretter of my morow gyft, throw grace of my fone ;
þis bere in his barnhede fall byde mony noyes."

And þen thomas femblife fone feyue ſkore maſons ;   *He gets 140 masons, and free-stone, as the Boar may want the towers to rest in, and finishes it.*
68 And feche fre ſtane out of A fer erthe.
"I fall bygge it," quod beket, "agayne the bere Ryse ;
If he hynttis ony harme as he hydder wendis,
At he may Reſt þerin, wyth his Rethe tuſkis.
72 þat man fall be makleſs, for mercy hime folows."

And þus is thomas toure mayde, þe mare is his myrthte ;
Of his maſons was mony wytht, he thame qwhittis.
He fayris in A fayre felde, and his folke hime folowys ;
76 And walkis be A wodefyde, and wonderly he ſpekis :
"Maſons, for Sant mary lufe, helpe at your mythttis,   *Then he bids his masons build three crosses ;*
That here were A fayre croſſe founded on this grunde ;
And downe in yhon depe dale dythtis ane oþer ;
80 And on yhone banke, whare yhone vynes growis, makis þe thride.
Fore the kynge of france wyſte qwhat wonder fulde be wrothte,
He walde þat A watter, or a well, hayd wecht it away.   *at the first of which the King of*
At þis croſſe þat is cleyn, is croune falle he loſſe ;

¹ A word is here lost.

26 POEM ON THOMAS A-BEKET'S PROPHECIES.

France shall lose his crown;
 84 And all fraunce vn to Sexty wynter efter.
  Þat ſo wonderfull wyes, and ſoe fewe þat þer is,
  Þat all the warlde ſwlde wyte be the wyll of our lorde.

at the second, bishops and prelates shall die;
  At yhon ſecunde croſs þat I of ſay ſchall,
 88 Byſchopis, Arſbiſchopis, abbottis, and priouris,
  And preloettis of haly kyrke, ſall þar lyffis loſs.

[Fol. 29a.] at the third cross the crown shall fall to the ground.
  At yhone thride croſſe, þen thripis all my ſhillis,
  Þe ſonne ſall forſake þe fadre; and þat is a Selly;
 92 And the croune be kelede to þe erthe wytht a knyghte;
  A batell of berdles barnes bring ſall it oure."

Lord Waryn's son jeers at Beket for his prophecy.
  Þone lawghis þe erlys ſonne of Waryne, & Iwis ſweris,
  "Was neuer wye of þis warlde þat durſt wakin ſlike bourdis,
 96 Her to Feght, no to feche the fayr honour of Fraunce.
  Qwha durſt buſk to Bolane, wytht ony brycht helmis?
  Or care on to calaſe, wytht ony cleyne cheldis?
  Ilk a lorde in the lande hume fore þe cheffe haldis."

Beket rebukes him.
 100 Thomas grewes at the gome, all if he gret were;
  "Þow gaffe me lytyll, be our lorde; leys the to ſay.
  It is trew, and no truffle, þat þis buk tellys;

The Boar shall tumble up France,
  For A tuſke of this bore ſall tumble vp þis lande;
 104 And a body ſall byde in A burghe, þat londyn is hattene,
  And nocht bryſt A briſſe of his bare Rygge.
  Serttes," ſays thomas, "her is a mor Selly!
  He ſays he ſall to the ſee, wytht A ſadde pepill;

root among walls, eat lords' bodies.
 108 And wrotte emong walles, and werke feell wonderys;
  And paſture hime propirly on proude lordis bodyes.
  Þar ſalbe no hatell, þat at hume huntis,
  Þat wythtoutyne hurte ſalle chape.
 112 He ſall lewe of his layke, ſo lell ſal be his hert;
  Bot he ſall clayme his comonys throw out all fraunce.
  All cretoye ſall haue care, when he furth caryes;

work wonders by the Seine,
  And be the watter of ſayne ſall Sellyes be ſeyne.
 116 Wyld wyis of wales ſall wyrk feell wonderys;
  And gomes of gourlande ſall get vp þar baneris,

burn Abbeville, and slay its men.
  And ſtyſſ knychtis ſtrek doune þar ſtremys.
  Abfyle for his boſt ſall balfully be brunt;

120 And ledys lofe þar lyffis þat to þat toune langis.
And in A foreft I fynde fall feell knychtis de ;
Ande the beft of beein fal by, when þe bayr bufkes,　[Fol. 29b.]
Fra his tufkis begynnes to tuyll, his tene falbe þe leffe ;
124 He fall grynne quhar he gafe, & grace fall him folowe ;
Ande þe fays put to þe flycht, þat þe floure berys,
And do hime draw to Sant denyfe, for drede of þe bare.
This ber falbe bufkede in A banke fyde,
128 Ande nocht fter A bresse for all þare ftern werdis.
Ande þen may Mount Joys murne, ande oþer moo cetefes ;　For this Boar may Mountjoy mourn;
Perty properly put downe for euer.　Caen and Calais,
Cane ande calyfe kepe þi turne, for þan þi care Ryfes !
132 Hogge fall full carfully be cast to the grunde ;　Hogge and Valois too;
Valoys, wythtoutyne fale, fall fall to the erth.　no house shall be left standing.
In quhyte fande the ledene fal be, 'no houfß lewyde.'
þe bare fall bufk to calyfe, wyth his brode bryffes,
136 Ande dere Inglande dyght þe, ande kepe well þi briffes !
A noyntede kynge fall come fro the North,　A king from the North shall invade the Boar's realm,
Ande noy hyme Ryght Ryght . . . . . ¹
Ande Ryde in the bares Royalme, þogff he no Rycht have.　but he shall
140 Bot he falbe hynte wyth a handfull ; his herme falbe þe more,　be caught and held prisoner.
And claughte on A clerke laide, þat Cutbert is [called],
And falbe lede to lond, þogh lothe thinke
þat Renk to Reft hime þar Rycht mony yheris ;
144 þat neuer was of this warlde fall wete qwhare he worthede.
Bot as A flomerande flepe war flongyn in his Erys,　The Boar shall rest till his tusks are grown; shall be stirred up by Berwick;
Un-tyll his gryfly tufkis be fo grete growene,
þat all the dukis wnder dryghtene fall drede hime allone.
148 He falbe waknede wyth A burghe that Berowyck hatte ;
And wander in A winter tyme wyth full wale knychtis.
þis kene wythtoutyne counter fall agayne care,
And fyne be comforth wyth A crowne, as criftis wyll Is.
152 He fall grife tyll hime his grym griffes, grathly hym felwene,
Ande ftable his ftiffe Roailme wyth fterne knyghtis,　[Fol. 30a.]

¹ Here seems to be some omission.

28 POEM ON THOMAS A-BEKET'S PROPHECIES.

assemble his knights, set sail, Ande nyghe tyll A nawy, his enmyse to noye ;
Ilka sarfyne may haue fyte quhen he to fchipe gang*is*.
and fight a battle at Boulogne. 156 At bolane fall byd hume A battell fulle hugge ;
Ande fyftyne hundreghe helmes þ*er* falbe hewene.
A byrde wytht two bek*is* bring fall full mony ;
Fyfty thowfande of fere pepyll fall folow his tayll,
160 To meke mary, ande a ber þat mekyll m*er*cy folowys,
Fro the bryde ande the bere be bufked in A felde ;
Syne fall come mony Sope, or els war ferly.
Thank God Benedicite !" fayde beket, ande bleffyt hime thr[i]ffe,
164 "That eu*er* fall A bare (as þis buk tellys),
a Boar can skip so. Skippe fo fleiftly, and he A fwyne lyk,
Qwhile lyonis, vnicorns, and liberd*is* Regnis !
Þan may ceteis haue cete, as the buk fays,
168 For the bere in lande haue laykede hime A ftounde.
Þai fall bane, that hime byd*es*, þat eu*er* he was borne ;
Yes, the Boar shall take Paris, For he to paryche paffe, wytht his Rout nobyll,
He fall tuche his tufk*es* tyll A ftone, þat mekyll ftrenth folow[ys],
172 And þai fall caft hime the keys our the clene yhatt*is* ;
and rule it, He fall Ryde throuch the Rych towne, Rewylle it hy*m* felvine ;
And brode buk*is* on breft*is* agaynis hume fall þai brynge.
It no wond*er*, Iwis, and ilka wye wyfte
176 Qwhat fall worth of his werk*is*, wythtin few yþ*er*is.
For hime behowes Semble, forfuth, þat lange has beyne fund[er],
Þe crounie, ande the thre nall*es*, & A fpere Rycht.
For all the blyffe of þat burghte, byde wyll he nocht,
and then attack the Bird with two beaks, [Fol. 30b.] 180 Bot eft*er* þe byrde wytht tw[o] bek*is* he wyll bufk.
Fray this bayre wytht his bryffes be bufkede in a feylde,
Þar beys na byerde wytht twa bek*is*, nor beft þat hede berys,
So hardy to lyght on þat lande, þar the ber Reft*is*.
who will not stand against him. 184 Þis byrde thar no3t treft on no tre, & he be anes turnede,
No perk hime on no pr*oper* perk wytht no proude pales,

For the Ryche bare wytht his tuſkes wyll Rywe þame *in
 ſonder,*
Ande he ſall [fight] ferſly xiiij. days in diu*erſe* places,
188 All gyffe he be wery, Iwis, and his wyes all.
Then ſhall he caſt vp his croune to the bleſſyt mary,
Ande beſek hyr of helpe, helle of all ſuccure :
He ſall be ware in the weſt whare A wye comes,   A knight shall come from the west.
192 A lefe knyght & A lene, wytht two long ſyd*is* ;
He ſalbe hardy, ande hathell, and her of hime ſelwyne ;
Lacede iij. libertt*is*, ande all of golde lyke,
Wytht A labell full lele, laide ewene our ;
196 A Rede ſchelde wytht A quhyt lyoune ſall c*um* fra the felde.
Melane, mak yow no myrth, for murne may yow ſwyth ;   Milan, Lombardy, and the three crowns shall the Boar win, and then sail
And lumberdy lely ſall lene tyll hume ſoun.
Þen ſall þis berde in his bek bringe thre crouns,
200 Ande bynde þame to this bare, beſt of alle othire ;
Þane þis bare ſall buſk tyll A brade watt*er*,
And on to ſant Nycholaß bowne hume fulle Soune ewine ;
& Redy his ſchippis, he that the ſoth tellys,
204 Wyth his pawelȝounis that is pr*oper*, and his prowude folk*is,*
To wende our the wane watt*er*, (& wyſſe hume our Lorde !)
And ſall fayr to Famagoſte, for-lyes to ſeke,   to Famagoste and Cyprus ;
And ſaill furth be cipres, as the buk tellis,
208 Ande Rynne up at Ryche Jaffe, (Joys to þame all !)   land at Jaffa,
To convert the cateff*es* þat noȝtt one Cryſt*is* lewys.
He is my contre-ma*n*, my *com*forth is the mor,
For he ſall lewe his trouth on cryſt*is* owyne grawde."   and reach Christ's grave (?)

212 Þen þerle ſone off w[a]ry*n* to thomas wend*is,*
"Þar ſall I feght fenely, be my fad*er* ſaule."   Lord Waryn's son [Fol. 31a.] says he will fight there.
"Þow ſwerys wond*er* Swyftly, & Swyppe may it eu*er* ;
Þat time of the ȝere, ande A tyde forþer,
216 May þow be laid full law, and all thi leue Armes ;
So þat no wy of this warlde ſall were þame on ſhuld*er*."
"Þat war a wond*er*," ſays the wak Rycht.   Beket says the land shall lose its lords,
"Lytyll land*is* lelely," ſays thomas, "ſalbe levyde."

F

220 Als leffe as þow þame thinkis, ... [1]
    þow falbe laide full law, and þow na lorde hade."
    þe gentyll fays, " be Sant mary! þat war gret murnyng,
    þat fuilk lordis of landis fwld fo law be layde ;
224 And no cofine vnder cryft þar caftels to welde."
    Then fays thomas, " In fathte, ferly is it none ;

and be ruled by females; or a pestilence shall come and desolate the land.
    þi land may far be famales, in fo Fer ȝeris ;
    Or þar may a peftellaunce proper fall in all landis,
228 þat may ger fexty cofins part wytht-in vij. wekis,
    And may mak mony Sorowles lykes, & joyles brydyles;
    And mak halykyrke to-trowlede, for tenyng of maryage ;
    And plewes to lygge wpon ley, þe larke lorde wax ;
232 And cateffis vnkyndly fall welde mekyll gudis ;
    þai fall forgette cryfte and his cleyne moder

Beket foretells the woes and wonders that shall befall,
    Qwhen thar Is no wye þat þis warld weldis.
    þen fall come A Snyll Snappyng to Swithe in þer hornes;
236 Hunger and hate warldles, I hythe þe for fuche,
    A wodenes to walk our þe landis, and þame wa wyrke,
    Bernes bundyn on to buredis and braydis full ȝarne,
    Tyll þai have knawyng of cryft and his bleffed moder.

till the people know Christ;
240 He fall paffe his courfȝ, and þat falbe well kennede,
    Ande do haly kyrke to heylde, I fay the for futhe,
[Fol. 31b.]
    To wend out our the wan watterys, as þar none ware ;
    It Sall Ryne Rede in the eft, and Rewth it is the mor.
244 And þen falbe wanttynge of wode, and wanyng of Irne ;

and wherever the Boar goes. Sir Edmund of Abingdon says it grows late.
    Suilk wonderys falbe wroucht whar the ber wendis."
    Edmound of abyndoun, þat Baroune all bleffede,
    Says, " my lorde, lelyli lythe me A ftounde :
248 The Sonne walkes weft, ande the day wendis ;
    þow tellys þame tales, þat trowys thame full lytyll."
    Ane angell bowed doune to beket in a blew wede,

An angel in blue bids Beket bind up his Book of Prophecies.
    And fayde, " binde vp thy buk, my lady the byddis."
252 And þen he hewed vp his handis, als he as he mycht,
    And lowes our lorde and his der moder

---

[1] The alliteration shows that half a line is omitted.

Off the talle that ſcho hume tould in the meene tyme.
Þen the buk was borne vp to þe blyſſe off our lorde;
256 And beket to burgone buſkes hume full Evine.

It is taken up to heaven, and Beket goes to Burgone.

Explicit.

IV.

ANCIENT SCOTTISH PROPHECY, No. 2.

[Fol. 32b.]
When the English priests have the Pope's power, strife shall arise.

Q When Rome Is removyde in to Inglande,
Ande the preſt haffys the poppys power in hande,
Betuix iij. and ſex (who ſo wylle vnderſtande),
4 Mekyll baret ande bale ſhall fall in brutis lande.
When pryde is moſt in price, ande wyt is in covatyſe,
Lychory is Ryffe, and theffis has haldin þar lyff,
Holy cherche is awleſſe, and Juſticis ar lawleſſe,
8 Bothte knychtis and knawys clede in on clethinge.
Be the yheris of cryſt comyn and gone,

In ninety-nine years

Fully nynty ande nyne, nocht one wone,
Þen ſhall ſorrow be ſettande vnſell,

Fortune shall turn the wheel, and loyalty reign.

12 Þan ſhall dame fortowne turne hir whell,
Scho ſall turne vp þat ar was doune,
And þan ſall leawte ber the crowne.
Betweyne þe cheyſſ of the ſomer & the ſad winter,
16 For þe heycht of þe heyte happyne ſall wer,
And everyche lorde ſhall auſternly werk;
Þen ſhall Nazareth noy welle A while,

The Lily shall hide his folk,

And þe lilly ſo lele wytht lovelyche flouris
20 For harmes of the harde heyte ſall hillyne his ledis;
Syne ſpeyde hime at ſped, and ſpawne in þe wynter;

and the Flowers in the Firth shall follow him.

All þe flowris in the fyrth ſall folow hime one;
Tat caldwers ſall call on carioun the noyus,
24 And þan ſall worthe vp wallys, and wrethe oþir landis;
And erth on tyll albany, if þai may wyne,
Herme wnto Alienys, aneuer þai ſall wakyne.

þe brutt*is* blude fall thame waykne & bryttne wy*th* brand*is*
of ſtell ;
28 Þar fall no baſtarde blode abyde *in* þat lande.
Þen Albanatt*us* þe kene, kynde kyng offe erthe, [Fol. 33*b*.]
Vnto þe libert ſhall leng, leve yhe non oþir.
The lyone, leder of beſt*is* . . . . . .
32 Shall lowte to þe libert and long hume wytht,   By Humber
And ſhall ſtere hume A ſtryff be ſtremis of humb*er*.   shall the Leopard deſtroy the
þe ſtepſonys of þe lyonne ſteryt vp at ones,   Lion's rebellious step-
þe leoperde fall þame ſtryke doune, and ſtroy þame for eu*er* ; sons,
36 He fall þame kenly kerſſe, as cryſt has hume bydyne ;
And þus he fall þame doune dryff ewyne to þe ende,
For þai luf nocht þe lylly, nor þe libert lelle.
And þai halde to þe harde, happyn as it may,
40 Ay to þe tayle of ſomyr tyne hir lappis,
Wytht þat fall A libert be louſe when þai leſt weyne.
Ane Egle of þe eſt, ande ane aventruſe byrde,   with the help
Shall fande flowrys to fange in þat fyrſte feſoun ;   of an Eagle of the East.
44 Sterte to þe ſtepſonys, ſtryke þame doune togeþ*er*,
To bynde bandis vnbrokyne þat ſalbe furthe broucht.
He fall hime [gather] garlandis of þe gay flowrys,
At in þat feſoune ſpredis fo fayre,
48 And all fall fawlo þe foulke þat þe freke ſtryk*is* ;
A fely northyrune flaw fall fadyne for eu*er*,   Afterwards,
Heraft*er* on oþir fyde forow fall Ryfe ;   sorrow shall rise :
þe barge of bariona bowne to the ſenkyne ;   laymen shall want spiritual offices.
52 Secularis fal fet þame in ſpir*it*ual clothis,
And occupy þar offices, ennoyntyd as þai war ;
Þar tonſurys tak wytht turnament*is* Inowe,
And trow tytylle of trouth þat þe ſtrenth hald*is* ;
56 Þat ſalbe tene for to tell the tende of þar forow,
Þat fall ourdryff the date doune to þe boke.
Þis moſt betyde in þe time, throw yhe for ſuthe,   This shall come to pass
Qwhen A, B, C, may fet hume to wryte.   in one thouſand three hundred and eighty- R.,
60 Anon eft*er* M¹ evene to Rewlle,
Tre CCC in A fute ſemblyt togeþ*er*,

[Fol. 34a.]

as Merlin
says.

Ande fyne eft*er* ane l, as þe lyne aſk*is*,
Tris X ande ane R ent*er*ly folowande;
64 Þis Is þe doloroufe date, under yhe þe gloſe,
Whereoff whyll m*er*lyne melys in his bok*is*.

Berwick! Be
glad of these
words that
Bede found;
thou shalt be
true to thy
king, the
Lion, for
ever.

Buſk ye wyell, Berwyk! be blyth of þ*is* word*is*
Þat Sant bede fande in his buk of þe byg bergh,
68 Þe trew towne vpon twede, wytht towrys fayre!
Þow fall Releve to þi keng þat is þe kynde Eyr.
Ande oþ*ir* burghys abowte, wytht þar brade wall,.
Sall wytht þe lyoune beleff, ande longe for eu*er*.

V.

SIX WISE MASTERS' SPEECH OF TRIBULATION.

HEre begynyth A ſhorte extracte, and tellyth how þar [Fol. 34b.]
ware ſex maſterys aſemblede, ande eche one aſkede
oþer quhat thing þai ſholde ſpek of gode, and all þei war
4 acordet to ſpek of tribulacoun.

The fyrſte maſter ſeyde, þat if ony thing hade bene mor I. There is
better to ony man lewynge in þis werlde þan tribulacoun, better; so
god wald haue gewyne it to his ſone. But he ſey wyell þat to Christ.
8 þar was no better, ande þarfor he gawe it hum, and mayde
hume to ſoffer moſte in þis wrechede worlde þan euer dyde
ony man, or euermore ſhall.

The ſecunde maſter ſeyde, þat if þar wer ony man þat II. It is
12 mycht be wyth-out ſpote of ſine, as god was, and myȝt levyn thirty years
bodely þirty yheris wyth-out mete, ande alſo were dewote ness, and
in preyinge þat he myȝt ſpeke wyth angele in þe erth, as with angels.
dyde mary magdalene, ȝit myȝt he not deſerve in þat lyffe ſo
16 gret meyde as A man deſervith in ſuffring of A lytyll tribulacoun.

The threde maſter ſeyde, þat if the moder of gode & III. Better
all the halowys of hewyn preyd for a man, þei ſhould not get and All
20 ſo gret meyde as he ſhould hymeſelfe be meknes and ſuffryng prayers.
of tribulacoun.

The fourth meſter ſeyd, "We werſchipe þe croſſe, for our IV. We
lorde Iheſus cryſt heng þer upon bodyly, bot I ſay we ſhoulde ship the cross
24 raþr, and be more Rycht ande Reſon, have in mynde þe
tribulacoun þat he ſuffreyde ther-vpon for our gylt and
treſpaſe."

The fyfte meſter ſeyd, "I had lever, and I myȝt be of V. It is
better than

THE MERITS OF TRIBULATION.

<small>all worldly goods,</small>
<small>[Fol. 35a.]</small>

28 ſtrenght and power, to ſuffer þe left peyn and tribulacoun
þat he ſuffrede here in erth, wyth mekness in herte, þan þe
meede or rewarde of all worldly godes; for Sant peter ſeyth,
'None is worthy to have tribulacoun bot þo þat deſyre it

32 wyth clene harte and wythoutyn errore;' for tribulacoun

<small>for it quenches ſin, and dis-closes God's secrets.</small>

quenchith ſynne, and it lernyth A man to know þe priveteis
[of] god, ande tribulacoun makyth a man to know hime ſelff
and his eyn cryſtyn, and it multyplieth vertuys in a man, ande

36 pergyth and clengyth hyme as fyre dothe goulde."

<small>VI. God is with those who bear it meekly;</small>

The ſext meſter ſeyd, "Qwhat man þat mekly in harte
ſofrythe tribulacoun, gode Is wyth hime, and beryth it hewy
charge of tribulacoun. And tribulacoun byeth ageyn tyme

40 þat is lofte, ande houldyth a man in þe way of rychtfulnes:
and of all yhiftes þat gode yevith to man, tribulacoun is beſt
& þe moſte worthy yhifte: alſo it is treſour to þe wich no

<small>it joins a man's soul to God. But we bear it badly for our little love to Christ.</small>

man may make compariſon: and tribulacoun Ioyneth a

44 manis ſoule to god: but quhat is þe cauſe we ſuffyr it þan
wyth ſo ewyll wyll? Thus it Is anſwerde ande ſeyd, for
thre thinges: The fyrſt thing, for we have letyll luffe to our
lord Iheſus cryſt. The ſecunde is, for [we] þenk lytyll of

48 þe gret meyde and profyte þat comyth þerof: The threde,
for we think lytyll or not of þe better peynes & grete
paſſyon þat our lord Iheſus cryſt ſuffrede fore ws in þe
Redemyng of oure ſynnes, and for to brynge vs tyll his

52 blys þat neuer ſhalle haue ende. A-m-e-n.

NOTES.

A.

Page 1, l. 3. *for law of god in document*, i.e. for teaching God's law. 11. *miserabilly*, this word is apparently written in mistake for *mesurabilly*. The adjective occurs in 53 and 116 with the more usual orthography.

P. 2, l. 22. *variance*, perhaps miswritten for *variante*, i.e. variable, as the word must be an adjective. 23 *is nocht to leff behynde*, apparently the construction is, It is not (a thing) to be left behind, i.e. neglected cf. infra. 191, where, to nowmer=to be numbered. 33. þᵉ should be *it*. The sense is: As the fire through redhot brands wastes itself, so the spendthrift is desolate. 36. The sense is, Examine thoroughly the purpose of thy servants to have it plain, so that thou mayest perceive if they be against thee, who have governance of thy goods in their hands.

P. 3, l. 58. *þat lefys by temporance*, i.e. that neglect temperance. The meaning of the whole is : To spend money on such men, with the idea (*proponande*) that thy goods should reestablish such foolish men in worship, let be, i.e. don't attempt it.

P. 4, l. 72. It certainly leaves them not till death sever them. 87. And therefore beware in thine expense ever to judge fairly between the purse and the appetite.

P. 5, l. 97. Therefore choose liberality (as a mean between gluttony and avarice), and leave them both; for liberality can spend at the right time, and without harm. 105. *þat he may wyne*, i.e. that which he may win. 107. *to oþir*, i.e. for others. 111. *Se be na way*, Take care that by no means.

P. 6, l. 122. For he (thy foe) is not always vanquished with the sword, but oft he is overcome by love, charitable deeds, and lowliness. 125. *Ber þe ewynli*, behave thyself without fickleness. 135. *of case*, perchance. 140. His truce is merely taken till his opportunity comes.

P. 7, l. 145. Nor is there leech who by any science can abate the annoyance of her that is a man's mate. 149. *and mare sobyr, &c.*, and make thee more calm to put up with such wickedness. 155. Which (i.e. sin) comes to them by kind and nature from Eve their foremother. 157. The sense seems to be: Thou shalt sooner stop the troublesomeness of froward women then when they chide and grumble by laughing (*for to lacht*) than to beat them with staves while they lie by thee awake. 162. *lef hir mys*, leave off from her wrong doing.

P. 8, l. 181. *Bot erare, &c.*, But sooner, my son, force thyself with all thy might, etc. 188. *Na in hym says*, Than in him (who) says. In the succeeding part of the sentence I fail to see the construction, and think there is an error. The sense is: I am to be relied on to treat my property as though it were my friend's as much as mine. 191. There are many friends as far as words go.

P. 9, l. 198. But give one pleasant word in return for another. 217. He shall have a wife whose name shall be poverty.

P. 10, l. 225. *Pryseis*, i.e. they prize. The lines mean: They esteem the laughter as a precious gift made to them, for it encourages them. 237. But get rid of that servant, as (thou wouldst of) enemies who wish thee no good. 240. *Thow felis*, i.e. thou feelest, perceivest; here used parenthetically: Those which are in their language (thou perceivest) flattering. 245. For whether thou work unrighteously or well, etc. 248. *with his mysdeide*, at his misdeed.

P. 11, l. 254. And wots well, before he goes, that he will not get you what you ask for. 264. *þi cowatynge exspire*, put an end to thy longing. 268. *bydyne of sellyn*, awaiting a sale.

P. 12, l. 280. They will take offence at you if you apply to them. 286. *Til hym geffis*, to him (who) gives. 292. When you are in the company of mighty men. 300. I am not at all clear about the meaning of this and the two following lines. *Thow* should apparently be *Throw*, i.e. through.

P. 13, l. 307. And sometimes he is an ape to make mows like a fool, but when he tumbles into a pool he is like a sow. 309. Dost

NOTES.   39

thou perceive thyself lightheaded from wine and over-exhilarated? 311. *beek þi nape*, bask thy nap, i.e. take a short sleep.

P. 14, l. 340. *and þu þe pane*, if thou takest pains. 345. But less frequently wilt thou separate misfortune from idleness, which had rather die than work. 350. But lies still till God comes and lifts him up.

P. 15, l. 360. And then blame fortune while thou thyself art guilty. 364. *þow ded*, i.e. when thou art dead; these words are used absolutely. The sentence means: Commit thy soul to God while alive thyself, rather than when thou art dead leave thy son to do it (by providing masses for its deliverance from purgatory), cf. infra, 370. 368. *one hee*, on high. 370. *Bandis*, here, the pains of purgatory.

P. 16, l. 382. Many times the son removes to a strange place. 386. *Stalynge*, making common, and here used for sending children into the world to earn their living, and guide themselves by their grace.

P. 17, l. 406. Such foolish women may blame their own wantonness, that cannot live in enjoyment by themselves. *þam alane* is here a case absolute.

B.

P. 18, l. 20. *lordly sall lythe*, I can make no better sense of these words than "he shall soothe or assuage (the press) in a lordly manner."

P. 19, l. 29. *Be þar*, i.e. (close) by that place. 33. *In als sall be tane*, als=halse, so that the meaning is, "shall be caught in a tight grip or embrace." 37. *Tro*. In some copies of the prophecy this is written *Troy*. 59. *A corde*, i.e. A-corde, accord, agreement.

C.

P. 23, l. 7. *For the falssede sall fayr, etc.* The falsehood shall run its course, etc. 16. And said to Earl Waryn's son: It is all good and a great recompense.

P. 24, l. 45. *gyff ony tuyll rase*, in case any trouble arose.

P. 25, l. 57. *Bot what wy, etc.* But whatever man wins it, let him cause it to be wrought himself. 69. *Agayne the bere Ryse*. To be in readiness when the Boar shall rise. 81. *Fore the kynge*, etc., for (if) the king of France knew, etc.

P. 26, l. 90. *þen thripis all my shillis*, then all my wisdom asserts: *Shillis* in this sense does not occur in the Glossaries; but a word in illustration occurs in Mr. Small's Metrical Homilies, p. 159:—

" For bathe thir foules haues crowding
Insted of sang, and stille murning,
And bitakenes that sinful man
That *schilwisnes* and insyt can,
Suld af this fules bisenes take,
To murne for his sin and sake."

100. Perhaps this means, "Thomas looks with horror at the man, mighty although he was." 101. *leys the to say*, leif is (me) to say to thee, i.e. I am glad to tell you.

P. 28, l. 169. They who await him shall ban the day that he was born.

P. 29, l. 188. *all gyffe*, all if, i.e. although, cf. supra. 100. 190. *helle of all succure*, hiding place (and therefore, storehouse) of all succour. 214. *Swyppe may it ever*, there is ever a chance of sudden change.

GLOSSARY.

N.B.—The letters A. B. C. D. and E. are used to distinguish the five separate pieces in the order in which they are printed.

Acordet, agreed, E. 4.
Alienys, aliens, D. 26.
Alkyne, of every kind, A. 20.
Als, also, B. 136.
And, an, if, A. 128; C. 38, et sæpe.
Anerly, solitary, C. 23.
Arch, purse. Lat. arĉa, A. 272.
Argewis, argues, A. 249.
Arthe, hearth, A. 92.
At (relative), that, D. 47.
Aucht, owned, C. 52.
Austernly, harshly, D. 17.
Aventruse, adventurous, D. 42.
Avyoune, } Avignon (?), C. 13,
Auoyoune, } 20.
Awale, value, A. 116.
Awnter, adventure, peril, B. 86.
Awtenyk, misprint for *awtentyk*, authentic, A. 1.

Ball, bale, B. 32.
Ballungerys, a kind of ships, B. 116.
Bane, to ban, to curse, C. 169.
Banftre, Banister, B. 54.
Baret, fighting, contention, D. 4.
Bariona, Bar-Jona, St. Peter. "The barge of Barjona" is "the vessel of the Papacy," D. 51.

Barnage, childishness, A. 50.
Barnagis, children, A. 386.
Barnhede, childhood, C. 66.
Bayre, boar, C. 50, 59.
Be, by, A. 111. *Et sæpe.*
Beande, being, A. 381.
Bedleme, Bethlehem, B. 14.
Beek, bask, A. 311.
Beme, trumpet (?), B. 71.
Ber, bier, B. 68.
Berdles, beardless, C. 93.
Bere, noise, B. 78.
Bernese, } barons, B. 21, 81.
Bernys, }
Bernyse, trappings, B. 18.
Best, beast, B. 30.
Better, bitter, E. 49.
Betwenſs, between, A. 85.
Beyne, been, B. 50.
Beys, is, C. 182.
Blat, blate, dull, blunted,
Blonk, a horse, perhaps originally white. F. blanc., C. 4.
Blycht, overjoyous, A. 309.
Bourdis, scoff, C. 95.
Braide, broad, C. 62.
Brattane, Britain, B. 8.
Brayde, to attack, assault, B. 30.
Brisse, } bristle, C. 105, 128.
Bresse, }

GLOSSARY.

Bunnys, prepares, B. 2.
Bushment, ⎫
Busment, ⎬ ambush, B. 21, 40.
But, without, A. 26, et passim.
By, buy, C. 6.
Bydyne, biding, expectation, A. 268.
Byg, ⎫ build, A. 257, 263 ; B.
Bygge, ⎬ 103.
Biggyne, building, A. 264, 267.
Byggod, built, C. 41.

Came, comb, B. 73.
Cayr, to search, seek, C. 21.
Ceteses, cities (?), C. 129.
Chape, escape, C. 111.
Chauner, to fret, grumble, A. 159.
Cheldis, shields. C. 98.
Cheſʒ, choose, B. 57.
Claughte, seizure, arrest, C. 141.
Clengyth, cleanseth, E. 36.
Cleyn, ingenuous, C. 43.
Compenſʒ, computation, measure, A. 358.
Consaffe, ⎫ conceive, perceive, A.
Consaife, ⎬ 37, 150.
Conserffe, conserve, preserve, A. 169.
Contene, regulate, A. 10.
Cordis, are suitable, A. 324.
Cosine, kinsman, C. 224.

Dale, dealing, A. 277.
Dantetht, delicacy, A. 334.
De, die, A, 346.
Dedit, possessed, A. 71.
Derrest, noblest, C. 52.
Dirke, dark, B. 50.
Disponeris, disposers, A. 330.
Dreſʒ, address, apply thyself, A. 291.
Dryghtene, lord, C. 147.
Dunbertone, Dumbarton, B. 124.
Dycht, prepare, C. 52.
Dyk, dig, A. 391.

Elderys, forefathers, A. 95.
Enterly, entirely, D. 63.
Enwcht, enough, A. 83.
Erare, ⎫
Erar, ⎬ sooner, A. 181, 186, 363.
Errer, ⎭
Ern, an eagle, B. 103.
Erth, to egg on, to incite, D. 25.
Eva, Eve, A. 156.
Ewynli, evenly, A. 125.
Eyn for evyn, equal, fellow, E. 35.

Fa, foe, A. 136, 167.
Falt, want, failure, A. 65.
Famel, family, A. 67, 82.
Familier, suitable for a family, A. 234.
Fande, proceed, go, D. 43.
Fane, fain, A. 270.
Fayis, ⎫ foes, A. 121 ; C. 125.
Fays, ⎬
Fecht, fight, A. 405.
Feell, many, C. 25, 28.
Felis, discernest, A. 240.
Fenely, fainly, with gladness, C. 213.
Fenȝeing, feigning, A. 204.
Fenȝit, feigned, A. 195.
Fere, appearance, show, demeanour, A. 195.
Ferlis, wonders, C. 25.
Festyn, feasting, A. 52.
Flech, flattering, A. 240.
Flettys, removes, A. 382.
Flurdowlyſʒ, fleur de lis, B. 117.
Flyt, quarrel, A. 404.
Foly, foolish, A. 26, 28.
Formodyr, fore-mother, A. 156.
Forsum, ⎫ to spend prematurely,
Forswme, ⎬ A. 108, 359.
Foulmert, ⎫ a weasel, B. 33, 74.
Fowmerte, ⎬
Founde, to go, B. 105.
Fre, fray, B. 31.
Frek, a strong man, B. 72.
Fremyt, foreign, distant, A. 382.
Freytt, freight, B. 46.

Ful, foolish, A. 406.
Fyld, field, B. 121.

Ganʒelde, profit, return for outlay, A. 328.
Gawe, gave, E. 8.
Gayis by, oversteps, A. 316.
Gayt-buke, goat-buck, B. 101.
Gef, if, A. 37.
Geff, if, A. 94.
Geffe, give, A. 83.
Ger, to cause, C. 57.
Ger, gear, possessions, A. 403.
Glowe, glove, C. 15.
Gomes, men, C. 117. A.S. guma, homo.
Grathede, prepared,
Grathly, readily, C. 152.
Grei, perhaps an error for *gret*, i.e., great, A. 194.
Grest, perhaps for, *greatest*, A. 288.
Grews, looks with horror, C. 100.
Gulosite, gluttony, A. 70.

Haffande, having, A. 211.
Haffe, have, A. 5.
Haffys, has, D. 2.
Haile, the whole, A. 79.
Hale, hall, A. 326.
Halows, leaves, hollow, empties, B. 1.
Halowys, saints, E. 19.
Hape, hope, A. 321.
Hate, hat, A. 282.
Hatel, i.q. hathell, a nobleman, C. 110, 192.
Hayd, had, C. 82.
He, } high, A. 42, 49, 267, 273.
Hee, }
Hele, health, A. 321.
Hende, kind, courteous, C. 37.
Hewed, heaved, lifted, C. 252.
Hewine, heaven, C. 40.
Hewy, heavy, A. 179.
Heycht, a promise, D. 16.
Heyte, heat, D. 20.
Hillyne, hide, D. 20.

Hude, hood, A. 282.
Hugge, huge, C. 156.
Hume, him, C. 5, et passim.
Hwndis, hounds, A. 327.
Hynge, hang, C. 59.
Hynttis, receives, C. 70.
Hythe, promise, C. 236.

Ientyll, gentle, C. 2.
Infekyt, infected, A. 70.
Inwy, envy, A. 127.
Irne, iron, C. 244.
Iuell, jewel, C. 1.

Joculary, the company of joculators, A. 216.
Ioculatouris, } idle triflers, A. 213,
Joculatoris, } 219.

Kelede, thrown, i.q. caled, see *Halliwell*. C. 92.
Kene, bold, C. 150.
Kennys, teaches, A. 258.
Koke, cock, B. 1.
Kynt, Kent, B. 39.
Kytht, the character proper to any person, B. 76.

Labell, a tassell. *Huloet*. C. 195.
Lach, laugh, A. 223.
Lacht, laugh, A. 159.
Laffe, the rest, remainder, A. 294.
Laiffe, the rest, A. 6.
Largness, liberality, a mean between extravagance and avarice, A. 97.
Laykede, sported, C. 168.
Leawte, loyalty, D. 14.
Lede, people, B. 128.
Ledene; legend, inscription, C. 134.
Ledys, plural of lede. A.S. leod: a man, a person, B. 113; C. 120.
Leff, leave, A. 23.
Lefys by, disregard, A. 58.
Lell, loyal, B. 82, 86.
Leng, to belong, D. 30.

GLOSSARY.

Lest, to last, B. 94.
Lestande, lasting, A. 404.
Leuer, rather, A. 346.
Lewis, believes, B. 113.
Lewyde, left, C. 58.
Lewynge, lwing, E. 6.
Lewys (plural), believe, C. 209.
Ley, untilled ground, C, 231.
Leys, a contraction for *leif is*, dear is, C. 101.
Libert, leopard, B. 13.
Liflate, livelihood, A. 385.
Loffys, praises, A. 244.
Louffe, Louse, } loose, B. 7; D. 41.
Love (*adj.*), dear, C. 6.
Lowes, praises, C. 253.
Lowte, to make obeisance, D. 32.
Lowynge, praise, A. 194.
Lukyne, protected (?), B. 126.
Lybberte, a leopard, B. 117.
Lykes, funerals, C. 229.
Lys, lies, A. 350.

Madyne, maiden, A. 318.
Make, mate, partner, A. 145.
Makleß, matchless, A. 194.
Makleß, mateless, without companion, A. 150.
Mane, man, A. 228.
Marmadyne, mermaid, B. 14.
Mater, matter, A. 206.
Melys, speaks, D. 65.
Merß, the eastern part of the Scottish border, B. 84.
Messanys, small pet dogs, A. 323.
Meyde, meed, E. 16, 20.
Meyne, Mene, } conceive, have in mind, B. 52, 55.
Miserabilly, measurably, in proportion to his means, A. 11.
Mistely, vaguely, A. 206.
Mistyr, necessity, A. 275, 279.
Mowis, grimaces, A. 307.
Mure, moor, B. 106, 107.
Myß, wrongdoing, A. 162.
Mythtt, might, C. 77.

Na, than, A. 184, 188, et sæpe.
Na, nor, A. 202.
Nam, name, A. 255.
Nape, a short time, A. 307, 311.
Not, naught, E. 49.

On, one, D. 8.
One, on, as one hee, on high, A. 368.
Our, above, A. 294.
Ourese, oversee, A. 43.
Ourseynge, A. 46.
Oynde, end, B. 100.

Paffe, pace, journey, C. 29.
Paweljounis, pavilions, C. 204.
Persaweis, perceivest, A. 309.
Pese, peace, B. 44.
Perk (n. and v.), perch, C. 185.
Plet, entwined, A. 375.
Plewes, ploughs, C. 231.
Poppys, pope's, D. 2.
Proffe, prove, B. 22.
Proponande, proposing, A. 59.
Pule, pool, A. 308.
Puppede, puppet, B. 35.
Pur, poor, A. 114, 118.
Purete, Purte, } poverty, A. 100, 217.

Quhik, quhilk, which, A. 215.
Quhillumys, sometimes, at times, A. 219.
Quhy, why, A. 102.
Qweynis, queens, A. 324.
Qwhittis, requites, pays, C. 74.

Rar, B. 96.
Rawne, Raven, B. 75.
Rechis, raches, dogs that hunt by scent, B. 119.
Renk, warrior, hero, C. 143.
Rethe, fierce, C. 71.
Rown, to whisper, B. 75.
Ruee, *for* reue, rive, tear, plunder, B. 87.
Rug (In the phrase *to rug and*

GLOSSARY. 45

rive), to plunder, to ravage, B. 81.
Ruke, Rook, B. 75.
Ruſs, to extol, to boast of, A. 184.

Sade, firmly set, A. 222.
Sadilles, saddleless, B. 18.
Saffage, outrageous, A. 300.
Sale, shalt, A. 346.
Salusyng, salutation, greeting, A. 19.
Sary, sorry, grievous, A. 76.
Saſell, ? C. 7.
Sayande, saying, A. 17.
Schir, } Sir, A. 252, 305, 314.
Schyr, }
Schoſe, chosen, B. 66.
Schowris, pangs of anguish, A. 377.
Secularis, secular persons, apparently here laymen, not secular priests, D. 52.
Secke, seek, A. 390.
Seldyne, seldom, A. 343.
Seldinar, more seldom, A. 345.
Sele, happiness, A. 246.
Selly, happiness, C. 17, 18.
Sellyn, selling, A. 268.
Semblise, assembles, C. 67.
Senkyne, sinking, D. 51.
Ser, several, many, numerous, A. 147.
Sertane, certain, A. 61.
Servandys, servants, A. 35.
Seseit, deposited, A. 290.
Settande, setting, waning, disappearing, D. 11.
Sey, saw, E. 7.
Slaar, slayer, A. 114, 229.
Sle, sly, A. 242.
Sleistly, nimbly, C. 165. Perhaps a clerical error for *sleifly*.
Slewcht, sloth, A. 338.
Slomerande, slumbering, C. 145.
Slongyn, coming lazily over (?), C. 145.
Snyll, keen, sharp, C. 235.

Sofrythe, suffereth, E. 38.
Sope, a crowd, multitude, C. 162.
Spelk, speak, B. 38.
Spensys, expenses, A. 53.
Sper, enquire after, seek, A. 164.
Stable, establish, C. 153.
Stalynge, dispersion (?), A. 386.
Sterne, stars, B. 14, 31.
Steryt, stirred, D. 34.
Stob, a stump, but here apparently used in the sense of *stumpy*, as an adjective, B. 107.
Stone, stolen, C. 3.
Swernes, laziness, A. 346, 347.
Swlde, should, C. 86.
Swycht, clear away from anything, A. 310.
Swyppe, to undergo sudden change, C. 214.

Takyne, token, A. 130.
Tane, taken, A. 255, et sæpe.
Tende, the tithe, the tenth part, D. 56.
Teyne, teen, sorrow, B. 98.
Theffis, thieves, D. 6.
Thole, tolerate, A. 236.
Thyne, thin, weak, A. 153.
Trast (v.), to trust, A. 197.
Trewis, truce, A. 140.
Tro, troth, faith, B. 37.
Truffle, deceit, C. 102.
Tume, time, B. 98.
Tumleſs, tumbles, B. 134.
Tuyll, trouble, tumult, C. 45; also as a verb, to trouble, C. 123.
Tyl, to, A. 36, et sæpe.
Tyne, to lose, B. 104.
Tynt, overthrown, lost, B. 91.
Tytylle, title, D. 55.
Þa, they, A. 37, 65.
Þan, then, A. 158.
Þat, that which, A. 105.
Þir, those, A. 190.
Þoch, though, although, A. 20.
Þogff, though, C. 139.

Vaike, weak, A. 13.
Varldly, worldly, A. 4.
Vawes, for *voustes*, he boasts, B. 79.
Vele, well, A. 245.
Verde, has been, A. 392.
Vesy, to visit, A. 216.
Vnkyndly, not connected by kinship, C. 232.
Vnsell (*adj.*), unhappy, D. 11.
Vofule, woeful, A. 73.

Waa, wo, C. 55.
Wachmane, watchman, B. 110.
Wacht, awake, A. 160.
Wadis, ? B. 41.
Wakin, waken, arouse, stir up, C. 95.
Wakyr, watchful, A. 168.
Wald, to be busy, A. 351.
Wale, value, A. 278.
Wale, excellent, C. 149.
Walkyr, wakyr, watchful, A. 355.
Wanfourtowne, misfortune, A. 345.
Wanwyt, senselessness, A. 400.
Wecht, washed, C. 82.
Wederys, weather's, C. 8.
Welany, villainy, A. 207.
Wencuste, vanquished, A. 122.
Wer, war, A. 404.

Wer, ware, cautious, A. 89.
Wesy, visit, A. 212.
Wetale, victual, A. 110.
Wete, to know, learn, C. 38.
Wnganand, unthrifty, A. 332.
Wodenes, madness, C. 237.
Worghe, in the phrase Waa worghe wo worth, C. 55.
Wouff, wolf, B. 110.
Wroke, spite, C. 10.
Wrothte, wrought, C. 81.
Wrotte, to root, C. 108.
Ws, us, B. 45, et sæpe.
Wy, Wye, } man, C. 57, 85, 95.
Wyell, well, E. 7.
Wygh, Wyghe, Wyghte, Wycht, Wytht, } with, B. 12, 18, 29, 32 47, et passim.
Wyne, winning, income, A. 180.
Wysse, to guide, C. 11.
Wyt, blame, A. 360.

Yheris, years, D. 9.
Yhifte, gift, E. 43.

ʒattis, gates, B. 3.
ʒeit, yet, A. 232.

The manufacturer's authorised representative in the EU for product safety is Oxford University Press España S.A. of El Parque Empresarial San Fernando de Henares, Avenida de Castilla, 2 - 28830 Madrid (www.oup.es/en or product.safety@oup.com). OUP España S.A. also acts as importer into Spain of products made by the manufacturer.

Printed and bound by CPI Group (UK) Ltd, Croydon, CR0 4YY

20/03/2026

02075338-0002